CONSUMER LESSONS
FROM A PANDEMIC

CONSUMER CORNER SERIES
UNCONVENTIONAL LESSONS FROM CONSUMER BEHAVIOR

Why do consumers make the choices they do, and what can those choices teach us? The Consumer Corner series explores the subtle forces that shape consumer behavior, across topics that range from food, retail, health, vacations, and more. By spotlighting overlooked, counterintuitive, or nontraditional insights, the series challenges standard economic thinking and highlights the messy, human side of decision-making that sometimes occurs when humans engage in the marketplace. Drawing on behavioral science, lived experiences, and industry expertise, this series reveals what people can teach us as they make complex choices across the supply chain.

SERIES EDITOR

Nicole J. Olynk Widmar
Professor and Head of the Department Agricultural Economics
Purdue University

OTHER TITLES IN THIS SERIES

Decisions That Shape Supply Chains
Markets We Thought We Knew

CONSUMER LESSONS FROM A PANDEMIC

NICOLE J. OLYNK WIDMAR
MICHAEL L. SMITH
ERIN ROBINSON

Purdue University Press
West Lafayette, Indiana

CONTENTS

INTRODUCTION

Consumer Lessons From a Pandemic

O ne of the fascinating things about decision-making is that we do it all the time yet we think shockingly little about it. What time to leave the house for work, what to eat for lunch, what to wear—and that is all before you walk out the door in the morning. Part of the reason we don't spend much time thinking about how we make decisions is because we tend to focus on outcomes rather than the decisions themselves. Every decision is made under risk; we cannot guarantee outcomes of much, if anything. As the saying goes, even the best-laid plans often go awry. The reality is, we can make the best choice, take the unarguably optimal path, do all the "right" things, and still encounter a completely unexpected outcome. Natural disasters, economic shocks, or even a global pandemic can dramatically change what results from our choices. This happens in our professional lives, of course, but also in our roles as consumers or household decision-makers, managing or influencing the consumption patterns of others.

Realistically, every decision is made under risk. And yet we rarely acknowledge, let alone account for it. Even if we wanted to, some events fall so far outside our usual expectations that they escape our planning entirely. Public health professionals and disease modelers had long discussed the potential for a respiratory pandemic, but for most people, the arrival of COVID-19 came without warning. Professionally, it changed how we sourced and supplied goods. Personally, it disrupted something as mundane as ordering groceries—and not foreseeing that milk in gallon containers was sold out while all other sizes sat untouched. Parents everywhere might be accustomed to planning ahead to avoid running out of the favorite snack of the month, but that's a short-term contingency plan (generally a week or two). Few (if any) had prepared for months of stay-at-home orders.

At the end of the day, consumer behavior is human behavior applied to consumption. We could just as easily consider producer decision-making under risk alongside consumer decision-making under risk. Both happen simultaneously whether you consider them that way or not.

Consumer behavior matters because producers create the goods and services we demand. But both production and consumption are much more complicated than we tend to admit. Raw ingredients must be sourced, moved, and delivered. Labor must be available at the right time, at the correct place, with the right knowledge and know-how. Add in other regulations, seasonality, biological limitations, and technical limitations, and only then do we arrive at production. Even after something is produced, it still must reach an awaiting consumer—at a price that is acceptable—through a purchasing channel that is accessible. Supply chains are complicated systems that most people thought very little about. Most of the time, they function so efficiently that we don't have to think about them at all . . . until the COVID-19 pandemic disrupted that illusion. It exposed the fragility of systems we had long assumed to be reliably resilient and made supply chains something everyday people started talking about.

1

HUMAN BEHAVIOR, BELIEFS, AND PRACTICES IN THE COVID-19 ERA

BY NICOLE J. OLYNK WIDMAR AND COURTNEY BIR

The COVID-19 pandemic altered everyday lives around the globe. Even individuals who were not directly affected—either health-wise or economically—could not ignore the massive societal changes that happened. What began as a public health crisis soon became a combined health and economic emergency, reshaping behaviors and influencing societies around the world.

Admittedly, public health messaging in 2020 was confusing. Responses to the pandemic, including recommendation practices to reduce viral spread (for example, wearing facial coverings or masks), became politicized.

Between June 12 and 20, 2020, we surveyed 1,198 US households to examine how COVID-19 affected their daily lives, personal values, and behaviors associated with reopening societally. We were primarily interested in household and personal impacts of COVID-19, perceptions of personal risks, and beliefs about masks and their use in preventing the spread of disease. Fundamentally, we sought to understand what respondents knew about the effectiveness of wearing masks in terms of disease control and

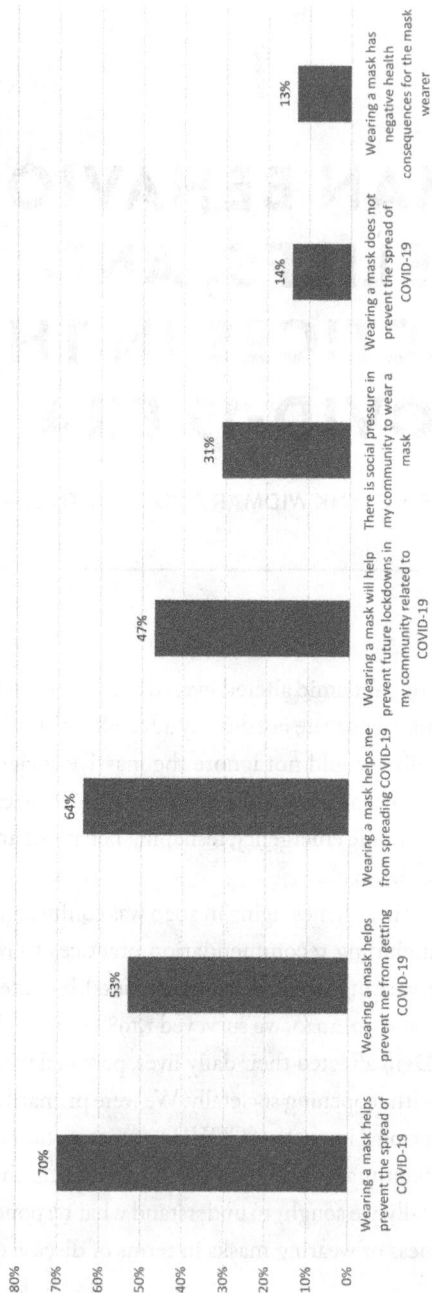

FIGURE 1.1. Percentage of Respondents Who Agree with the Following Mask-Related Statements. Created by Nicole Widmar and Courtney Bir.

whether they perceived the practice as an aid in preventing future shutdowns of their community, and thus their local economy.

Here's what we learned. At that time, we found that 83 percent (±3 percent) of respondents believed masks played some role in US society. To dig deeper into this perception, we asked respondents to indicate their level of agreement with a series of seven mask-related statements.

Interestingly, 70 percent of respondents correctly indicated that wearing a mask helps prevent the spread of COVID-19; 64 percent reported that wearing a mask prevents the wearer from spreading the virus. Yet, only 47 percent of respondents thought wearing a mask would help prevent future lockdowns in their communities, indicating a potential disconnect in individual behavior and community-level outcomes. This disconnect is worthy of future investigation, although the consequences of an individual's actions versus the collective community's actions and community-level outcomes is certainly nothing new societally.

Adapted from original posting as *ConsumerCorner.2020.Letter.12* (https://agribusiness.purdue.edu/consumer_corner/human-behavior -beliefs-and-practices-in-the-covid-19-era/)

2

A TALE OF TWO PETE'S

COVID-19 Impacts and Mask Usage Beliefs in Purdue Pete and Pistol Pete Territories

BY NICOLE J. OLYNK WIDMAR AND COURTNEY BIR

C hapter 1 introduced an ongoing research project dedicated to understanding COVID-19 household-level impacts and mask wearing behaviors by US residents. From its conception (April–May 2020) through data collection (June 2020) and analysis (June–July 2020), the project tracked "hot spots," or regions with rising case counts, around the country. This chapter shares the differences in perceptions and behaviors surrounding masks in different geographical regions during the COVID-19 pandemic.

When the fall 2020 semester came for Purdue University and Oklahoma State University, attention to mask usage in and around college towns had increasing real-time importance. This supplementary analysis compared perceptions and use of masks by residents of and around Purdue University's Boilermaker territory versus residents of and around Oklahoma State University's Cowboy territory. In other words, we explored how perceptions and use of masks in response to COVID-19 varied between two distinct geographic groups: the Indiana region (comprised of Indiana, Michigan, Ohio, Kentucky, and Illinois), against the Oklahoma region (comprised of Oklahoma, Kansas, Missouri, Arkansas, Texas, New Mexico, and Colorado).

Data were collected using an online survey from June 12 to June 20, 2020, as many US residents returned to public places. Respondents were sourced through Kantar (2020), a company with a large opt-in panel database. Participants were required to be at least 18 years of age. The research survey instrument was approved by Oklahoma State University IRB (IRB# 20-283). As COVID-19 spread is not impacted by state borders, this analysis took explicit account of states with shared borders, in recognition of the likely spillover effects from nearby states. For Purdue University, this included Indiana and its surrounding states: Michigan, Ohio, Kentucky, and Illinois. The remaining states were classified as non-Indiana and surrounding states. For Oklahoma State University, the grouping included Oklahoma and its surrounding states: Texas, New Mexico, Colorado, Kansas, Missouri, and Arkansas. All other states were classified as non-Oklahoma and surrounding states.

The results of demographic questions were compared between these state groupings and the surrounding states using the test of proportions (Acock 2018). Respondents were asked on a scale of 1 (not impacted) to 5 (impacted) the extent to which COVID-19 affected five different daily activities. The mean responses were compared between the states and the surrounding states studied and the nonsurrounding states using a *t*-test (Gosset 1908; Welch 1947).

Respondents answered the following question: "Do you agree that masks (meaning any face covering that covers your nose and mouth) have any role in US society related to the spread of viral disease, especially COVID-19, in the June–December 2020 time frame?" Answer choices included: (1) "No—they have absolutely no role whatsoever in US society" and (2) "Yes—they have some potential role in US society." Respondents were also asked a series of questions related to beliefs surrounding masks ranging from "Wearing a mask helps prevent the spread of COVID-19" to "Wearing a mask has negative health consequences for the mask wearer."

Respondents who believed masks had a role in US society were asked a follow-up set of questions regarding their mask-wearing behavior in specific locations. If respondents indicated the location was open in their community and one they visited, respondents then indicated whether they

(a) wore a mask voluntarily, (b) were required to wear a mask, or (c) did not wear a mask. Additionally, respondents rated agreement (1 = strongly disagree to 5 = strongly agree) with the statements: (1) someone in their household or that they frequently spend time with is at a higher risk of COVID-19 complications, and (2) they themselves are at higher risk. Mean responses for each group were statistically compared.

An Extension document summarizing the results was produced (Oklahoma State University 2020).

Before examining COVID-19 specific results, we compared demographics between respondents from Indiana and surrounding states versus the rest of the country, as similarly for Oklahoma and surrounding states. Table 2.1 summarizes these demographics, revealing Indiana and surrounding states were statistically less likely to have household incomes between $75,000 and $99,999 than the rest of the country. Respondents from Oklahoma and its surrounding states were more likely to be aged 18–24 and less likely to be 65 or older compared to the rest of the country.

Respondents from Indiana and surrounding states reported a lower perceived impact in their ability to find meat, milk, and perishable grocery items when compared to other activities and to the rest of the country. Respondents from Oklahoma and the surrounding states indicated they experienced a lower level of impact in their ability to find meat, milk, and other grocery items like paper products when compared to all other activities studied.

Table 2.3 quantifies the percentage of respondents in 2020 who agreed with various statements about mask wearing in the United States. Across all four respondent groups, the majority (79–84 percent) believed that masks had some role in US society related to slowing the spread of viral diseases, particularly COVID-19. However, regional variation was evident. A higher percentage of respondents from Indiana and the surrounding states believed that wearing a mask had negative health consequences for the mask wearer compared to respondents elsewhere in the country. Similarly, a lower percentage of respondents from Oklahoma and the surrounding states believed wearing a mask helped prevent the spread of COVID-19 and reduced the need for lockdown, compared to those in

TABLE 2.1. *Demographics for Indiana and Surrounding States and Oklahoma and Surrounding States (percent of respondents)*

DEMOGRAPHIC VARIABLE	INDIANA + SURROUNDING STATES, RESPONDENTS (N = 158)	NON-INDIANA + SURROUNDING STATES, RESPONDENTS (N = 1,040)	OKLAHOMA + SURROUNDING STATES, RESPONDENTS (N = 151)	NON-OKLAHOMA + SURROUNDING STATES, RESPONDENTS (N = 1,047)
Gender				
Male	41	48	47	47
Female	59	51	53	52
Age				
18–24	9	10	16*	9*
25–34	20	17	20	17
35–44	17	16	16	16
45–54	16	18	18	18
55–65	18	17	14	17
65+	18	20	14*	21*
Income				
$0–$24,999	31	23	25	24
$25,000–$49,999	28	24	24	25
$50,000–$74,999	16	19	18	18
$75,000–$99,999	8*	14*	13	13
$100,000 and higher	16	20	19	19

(continued)

TABLE 2.1. (*Continued*)

DEMOGRAPHIC VARIABLE	INDIANA + SURROUNDING STATES, RESPONDENTS (N = 158)	NON-INDIANA + SURROUNDING STATES, RESPONDENTS (N = 1,040)	OKLAHOMA + SURROUNDING STATES, RESPONDENTS (N = 151)	NON-OKLAHOMA + SURROUNDING STATES, RESPONDENTS (N = 1,047)
Education				
Did not graduate from high school	2	3	4	2
Graduated from high school, Did not attend college	34	28	32	28
Attended college, No degree earned	24	24	27	23
Attended college, Associates or bachelor's degree earned	30	31	25	32
Attended college, Graduate or professional degree earned	9	14	11	14

*Indicates the percentage of respondents from that category from that state and surrounding states is statistically different from non–that state and surrounding states at the < 0.05 level.

TABLE 2.2. *Mean Response on a Scale of 1 (not impacted) to 5 (impacted) for Respondents Who Did Not Respond That the Activity Did Not Apply to Them (i.e., they were never planning to travel in the first place)*

ACTIVITY	IN STATES	NON-IN	OK STATES	NON-OK
Respondent's daily activities outside of work/school	3.57a* N = 144	3.56a N = 962	3.38ab* N = 142	3.59a N = 964
Ability to buy paper products (e.g., toilet paper, paper towels)	3.62a N = 154	3.45a N = 1,018	3.16ac† N = 142	3.50a† N = 1,026
Ability to find meat, milk, and perishable grocery items	3.23b† N = 152	2.98b† N = 1,015	2.93c N = 147	3.02b N = 1,020
Ability to execute travel plans	3.66a N = 118	3.92c N = 817	3.72bd N = 127	3.91c N = 808
Activities related to respondent's work/school	3.60a N = 113	3.53a N = 767	3.52ad N = 125	3.54a N = 755

*Matching letters indicate the mean is statistically different down the column. For example, the mean for Indiana and the surrounding states for the activity respondent's daily activities outside of work/school is statistically different from the mean response for the activity ability to find meat, milk, and perishable grocery items but not statistically different from the activity ability to buy paper products at the < 0.05 level.

†Indicates the mean is statistically different between either Indiana or Oklahoma and surrounding states and either non-Indiana or Oklahoma and surrounding states for that activity at the < 0.05 level.

other regions. A higher percentage of respondents from Oklahoma and surrounding states also agreed with statements claiming that masks do not prevent the spread of COVID-19 and that they pose negative health consequences for wearers.

Table 2.4 explores mask-wearing behavior by location. Of the respondents who indicated masks had at least some societal role and who visited the location in person, individuals from Indiana and the surrounding states were more likely to voluntarily wear a mask at locations such as big box grocery stores, specialty grocery stores, home improvement stores, clothing stores, and other retail stores compared to their counterparts elsewhere. In contrast, Oklahoma respondents who attended these locations

TABLE 2.3. *Percentage of Respondents Who Agreed with Mask-Related Statements*

	INDIANA AND SURROUNDING STATES (N = 158)	NOT INDIANA AND SURROUNDING STATES (N = 1040)	OKLAHOMA AND SURROUNDING STATES (N = 151)	NOT OKLAHOMA AND SURROUNDING STATES (N = 1,047)
YES—masks have some potential role in US society related to the spread of viral disease, especially COVID-19	81*	83*	79*	84*
Wearing a mask helps prevent the spread of COVID-19	66*	71*	62*†	71*†
Wearing a mask helps prevent me from getting COVID-19	52	53*	45†	54*†
Wearing a mask helps prevent me from spreading COVID-19	65*	64*	55†	65*†
Wearing a mask will help prevent future lockdowns in my community related to COVID-19	44*	48	36*†	49†
There is social pressure in my community to wear a mask	28*	31*	31*	31*

| Wearing a mask does not prevent the spread of COVID-19 | 18^{*} | 13^{*} | $19^{*\dagger}$ | $13^{*\dagger}$ |
| Wearing a mask has negative health consequences for the mask wearer | $18^{*\dagger}$ | $12^{*\dagger}$ | $15^{*\dagger}$ | $12^{*\dagger}$ |

* Indicates the percentage of respondents is statistically different between those who selected they agreed with the statement and those who did not at the < 0.05 level. Those who did not select that they agreed with the statement and those who did sum to 100% within a category (i.e., Indiana and surrounding states) were not included for brevity with the exception of the role of masks in society.

† Indicates the percentage of respondents between the two levels within a category. For example, men *vs.* women or high total *vs.* not high total are statistically different at the < 0.05 level.

TABLE 2.4. Mask-Wearing Behavior Among Respondents Who Visited Each Location (percentage of respondents, n given in table)

| | PERCENTAGE OF RESPONDENTS | | | | | | | | | | | | | | | |
| | N | | | | I WEAR A MASK VOLUNTARILY | | | | I AM REQUIRED TO WEAR A MASK | | | | I DO NOT WEAR A MASK | | | |
	IN STATES	NON-IN	OK STATES	NON-OK	IN STATES	NON-IN	OK STATES	NON-OK	IN STATES	NON-IN	OK STATES	NON-OK	IN STATES	NON-IN	OK STATES	NON-OK
In-person religious service	43	282	49	276	65	50	43	54	23*	40*	39	38	19	16	27*	14*
Big box grocery store/supermarket	109	775	105	779	76*	61*	67	63	20*	37*	18*	38*	15	12	22*	11*
Specialty grocery store	81	574	77	578	74*	57*	69	58	30*	41*	25*	42*	11	11	14	11
Gym	29	207	46	190	65	47	37	52	31	37	39	35	14	23	33*	19*
Home improvement store	96	633	92	637	73*	58*	68	59	26*	37*	25*	38*	13	13	16	12
Restaurant	72	453	74	451	57	50	49	52	29	34	23*	35*	24	24	34*	22*
Workplace	58	405	70	393	52	41	36	43	53	51	49	52	12	20	23	18
School	27	172	32	167	70	53	59	55	37	40	41	39	4	14	16	12
Clothing store	79	499	79	499	73*	57*	66	58	21*	35*	20*	35*	15	16	19	15
Retail store other than grocery, clothing, or home improvement	101	653	94	660	71*	61*	65	62	22*	36*	20*	36*	18	13	21*	13*

*Indicates the mean is statistically different between Indiana and surrounding states and non-Indiana and the surrounding states for that location and column at the < 0.05 level. For example, the percentage of respondents from Indiana and the surrounding states who voluntarily wear a mask in a big box grocery store/super-market is statistically different from non-Indiana and the surrounding states.

TABLE 2.5. *Mean Response on a Scale of 1 (strongly disagree) to 5 (strongly agree) of Respondent's Level of Agreement with the Following Statements*

ACTIVITY	IN STATES (N = 158)	NON-IN (N = 1,040)	OK STATES (N = 151)	NON-OK (N = 1,047)
Respondent's level of agreement that someone in their household or that they frequently spend time with is at higher risk of complications of COVID-19	3.00	2.90	2.64*	2.95*
Respondent's level of agreement that they are at higher risk of complications of COVID-19	2.85	2.86	2.65*	2.88*

*Indicates the mean is statistically different between either the Indiana or Oklahoma and surrounding states and either non-Indiana or Oklahoma and the surrounding states for that activity at the < 0.05 level.

were more likely to report not wearing masks in person, particularly in religious services, big box grocery stores, restaurants, and other retail stores when compared to the rest of the country.

Understandably, individuals who are at higher risk of complications from COVID-19—or who frequently interact with such individuals—may have had heightened concerns about COVID-19 transmission. Table 2.5 quantifies the self-reported high-risk classification of respondents and those around them using mean agreement scores on a 5-point Likert scale, where 1 = strongly disagree and 5 = strongly agree.

Respondents in Indiana and surrounding states and the rest of the country did not differ significantly in their agreement levels. However, respondents from Oklahoma and surrounding states had a lower level of agreement with both statements, suggesting they perceived less personal or household risk related to COVID-19 complications.

WORKS CITED

Acock, A. C. 2018. *A Gentle Introduction to Stata*, 6th ed. Stata Press.

Gosset, W. S. 1908. "The Probable Error of a Mean." *Biometrika* 1–25.

Kantar. 2020. "About Kantar." https://www.kantar.com/about.

Oklahoma State University. 2020. "OSU Study Provides Insights into Regional Beliefs About Pandemic-Related Wearing of Masks." news.okstate.edu. July 23. https://news.okstate.edu/articles/agriculture/2020/stotts_mask-survey.html.

Welch, B. L. 1947. "The Generalization of 'Student's' Problem When Several Different Population Variances Are Involved." *Biometrika* 28–35.

Adapted from original posting as *ConsumerCorner.2020.Article.02* (https://agribusiness.purdue.edu/consumer_corner/a-tale-of-two-petes/)

3

CONSUMER SPENDING IS TODAY'S STATISTIC; CONSUMER BEHAVIOR IS FAR LONGER LASTING

BY TORRIE SHERIDAN AND NICOLE J. OLYNK WIDMAR

Remember when, back in March 2020, we talked about two weeks at home to "stop the spread" of COVID-19? Then we shifted to "flatten the curve" over a month or two. In hindsight, lockdowns did indeed help reduce transmission and avoid overwhelming hospitals, but these lockdowns carried a high cost financially and socially (Rebucci 2024). Despite all efforts, millions died during the COVID-19 pandemic.

What we initially saw as a short-term disruption became a defining era. From an economic and market perspective, this period triggered more than a temporary shift in household spending. It prompted lifestyle and behavioral changes, many of which outlasted lockdowns, and some persisted well beyond when pandemic restrictions lifted. From how we shop (such as online shopping for everything) to how we eat, COVID-19 changed consumer behavior in ways that continue to shape our daily lives).

EVERYDAY SHOPPING AND SPENDING

Have you ever poked fun at the stockpiling and pantry behaviors of an elder family member? You may want to rethink that the next time you step over your own stash of toilet paper and paper towels. The stress of the pandemic manifested in household spending, particularly on essentials such as food and daily use supplies. We saw notable shifts such as:

- Fewer but larger shopping trips
  - Not everyone could afford to stock up all at once. That meant more frequent trips for some, often when shelves were already bare. Even if there were funds, transportation challenges made it hard for some to haul home bulk items. In short, stocking up and prepping for disasters when it comes to groceries and household necessities is fraught with inequities, and while the advice to "have two weeks of supplies on hand" was somewhat of a one-size-fits-all recommendation, the reality of implementation is most certainly not.
- Stockpiling (okay . . . hoarding) nonperishables or long-shelf-life items
- Ordering in bulk
- Buying online what used to be bought in-store
- Curbside pickup or delivery for groceries
  - Speaking of curbside pickup, delivery, and other grocery-fetching mechanisms, how many of us have found a "new normal" in these services? Even post-pandemic, curbside and delivery remain part of everyday routines for many.
- Cooking at home
  - So. Many. Dishes. During lockdown, demand for meals at restaurants plummeted (Guszkowski 2021). Americans had long been growing their share of consumption outside the home, eating out at restaurants or eating on the go. As reported by *Fortune*, "In March, the USDA's monthly sales of food figures showed that money spent on food away from home (FAFH) had dropped from $67.6 billion in February to $54 billion in March, a 20%

decline, while sales of food at home (FAH) increased $62.9 billion to $79.3 billion, or 26%. But the real shift came in April, when more states were in serious lockdown. Spending on food away from home plummeted 34% over the previous month to $35.7 billion. That's less than half of what Americans spent on FAFH in December 2019" (Lambert and Kowitt 2020).

◦ As pandemic restrictions eased in 2021 and 2022, Americans began dining out again, but the restaurant scene looked different. Many offered more takeout food than they did before the pandemic; some shrank or eliminated dining rooms (Wiener-Bronner 2023). Seeking to reopen, other restaurants partnered with local officials to expand outdoor dining offerings as well (Bangert 2020). While some of these changes seem to stick for the long run (like expanded takeout service), other services like outdoor dining (which includes closure of streets) seem to have been curtailed by 2024 (Offenhartz 2024).

◦ The pandemic-era precautions undoubtedly had some sticky effects on human behavior. While most adults will recall the pre-pandemic world, our children may not. Reviews of how the pandemic altered our children's lives, specific to food, have found mixed effects: less fast food, but also less consumption of fruits and vegetables, more snacking, and indulging in sweets (Pourghazi et al. 2022). Anecdotally, we can report that there may be other behavioral effects. Anyone who's trained (I mean taught) a five-year-old to semi-appropriately behave in a restaurant knows that time away from those settings makes reentry harder.

Beyond groceries and toilet paper, what about the bigger ticket spending, like vacations during a pandemic? Vacation travel, annual visits to faraway family, and milestone events were altered, put on hold, or completely reimagined due to pandemic precautions. Some people traveled by car instead of flying, and some chose to stay home. Some people changed plans and stayed at the beach house or cabin longer, aided by working remotely or homeschooling. Some people attempted business as usual and traveled to distant locations with kids in tow, and others were horrified at the prospect. Regardless, a multitude of economic questions had to be addressed at the time, like these:

- Are we postponing or canceling?
- Should we reallocate that money to something else—or save it?

We also revisited the implications for spending on "goods vs. experiences":

- The *New York Times* reported on both pools and bicycles being extremely hard to find (Goldbaum 2020; Tully 2020). "Build your own summer fun at home" items flew off shelves.
- There had recently been movement toward spending on experiences pre-pandemic, but when those experiences were no longer available, did we move back toward buying "stuff"? Or are we postponing our spending for another day? Or are we still spending on experiences, but different experiences than we would have previously?
- COVID-19 also disrupted the "once in a lifetime" events that had to be reconsidered during the pandemic. Weddings. Honeymoons. Graduations. Sure, COVID-19 impacted how we lived our day-to-day lives, but we can't forget what it did to those monumental types of events. Many 2020 weddings were cancelled, postponed, and altered. Births were no longer celebrated with visitors at the hospital (Kanner 2020).

There was a fair amount of reporting on weddings, and for a bit it was becoming a thing to get married on Zoom (which is apparently legal in California and New York, although this is most certainly not intended as legal advice) (Schreiber and Kelly 2025). There are also a number of considerations about the birth of babies, many of which have been explored in the popular press and are related to the risk involved with bringing multiple people together in a medical facility and around newborn babies. Honeymoons—a high-spend trip that usually elicits the willingness to spend more, do more, and travel further—were also put on hold.

What happened to spending on the honeymoon when the wedding is cancelled or scaled down? In normal times, one might posit that wedding spending is reallocated to a longer or more elaborate honeymoon. Given travel restrictions and health concerns, that wasn't an immediate option; but when would it be?

Were newlyweds spending on durable goods instead? Did they get new cars or make down payments on houses instead of taking a honeymoon? Did they save instead of doing the big wedding and honeymoon, and are they forgoing the experiences altogether?

Case in point: Torrie (the contributing author of this chapter) married an accountant in December 2019—right before tax season. Their magical honeymoon would have to wait until after tax day in mid-April (before COVID influenced the change of tax day to mid-July). They were planning a getaway cruise out of the country to visit tropical islands, take part in adventurous excursions, and fill the days with activities from sunup to sundown. But that long-awaited cruise ship that was supposed to sail them away from postwedding and post–tax season stress went from dream vacation to pandemic hotspot. Needless to say, plans took an alternate course and they stayed on dry land.

Instead, Torrie and her spouse waited until late July. They opted to stay closer to home and out of the airports. Instead, they hopped in the car and went with another couple whose honeymoon plans were cancelled too. They split the cost of a rental house instead of booking a busy hotel filled with strangers, and while they would normally grocery shop at their destination, they shopped at home and packed as many groceries as they could into a cooler to avoid crowds and shopping at unfamiliar places. There were no big excursions or experiences aside from dinner at restaurants (wearing masks) and sitting socially distanced on the beach for a week.

While money was saved by taking an alternative trip, they still considered sailing off on a honeymoon cruise at a later point. Regardless, COVID caused us to spend our time, money, and efforts differently than we ever imagined on our once-in-a-lifetime events.

In the long run, we don't know if behaviors returned to normalcy or what sorts of changes we will continue to adopt or adapt. But some questions during the pandemic still linger:

- Will the sharing economy rebound? It was *very* much in vogue pre-pandemic, particularly among younger consumers who didn't necessarily want to own items they used infrequently. But sharing isn't simple in pandemic times. Even ride sharing and public transportation look a little different now, as many of us use our cars as personal bubbles in many settings with drive through and pickup everything.

- What about tiny houses and dense urban living? Little homes and itty-bitty big-city dwellings got awfully tight after a few weeks indoors. When you are never home, it makes sense to keep small spaces and live your life out in society, but when society sends you home and your home is built for sleeping and the occasional lazy Sunday afternoon, we rethink those living arrangements. Quarantine with children in the backyard running laps is very different from quarantine with children running laps in your apartment living room (perhaps without direct outdoor access), or without outdoor space of any kind if parks were closed where you live.

- If you are someone who now works remotely for the long haul, where do you want to do it? Seasonal rentals went up significantly in 2020 as people flocked to vacation locations to spend their time in spring and summer (Bedo 2020). That's already "in the books," as they say.

Today, remote work has solidified its place in the employment landscape. The shift has influenced residential patterns, with many employees relocating from high-cost urban areas to more affordable suburban or rural areas. Office vacancy rates are also changing, which has led to reevaluating office space needs.

In response to these trends, some countries have introduced programs to attract remote workers. For example, Barbados launched the "Barbados Welcome Stamp," allowing foreign visitors to work from home for up to one year in Barbados. There was even a family bundle option allowing families to bring their kids.

As remote work continues to evolve, its long-term effects on living arrangements, real estate markets, and urban development still remains in question.

WORKS CITED

Bangert, Dave. 2020. "Dining in Downtown Lafayette Streets Delayed One Weekend, Now Starts Aug. 28." jconline.com/story. August 18. https://www.jconline.com/story/news/2020/08/18/dining-downtown-lafayette-streets-delayed-one-weekend-now-starts-aug-28/3393055001/.

Bedo, Nicolas. 2020. "Seasonal Rentals Spike in Tourism Hotspots as Vacation Rental Hosts Wait Out COVID-19." realtor.com. May 20. https://www.realtor.com/research/seasonal-rentals-spike-in-airbnb-hubs-as-hosts-wait-out-covid-19/.

Goldbaum, Christina. 2020. "Thinking of Buying a Bike? Get Ready for a Very Long Wait." nytimes.com/2020. May 18. https://www.nytimes.com/2020/05/18/nyregion/bike-shortage-coronavirus.html.

Guszkowski, Joe. 2021. "How the Pandemic Impacted Restaurants' Spending." *Restaurant Business*. June 20. https://www.restaurantbusinessonline.com/operations/how-pandemic-impacted-restaurants-spending.

Kanner, Morgan Gibson. 2020. "The Knot's Official Guidebook for COVID-19 Wedding Help." *the knot*. December 23. https://www.theknot.com/content/covid19-help.

Lambert, Lance, and Beth Kowitt. 2020. "The Coronavirus Pandemic Is Dramatically Changing the Way Americans Eat." fortune.com. July 21. https://fortune.com/2020/07/21/us-consumer-spending-food-dining-out-restaurants-coronavirus-pandemic-lockdown/.

Offenhartz, Jake. 2024. "New York City's Freewheeling Era of Outdoor Dining Has Come to [an] End." apnews.com/article. August 6. https://apnews.com/article/outdoor-dining-nyc-eric-adams-882bea8068d2fc6e390c0b17c95405ca.

Pourghazi, Farzad, Maysa Eslami, Amir Ehsani, Hanieh-Sadat Ejtahed, and Mostafa Qorbani. 2022. "Eating Habits of Children and Adolescents During the COVID-19 Era: A Systematic Review." *Frontiers in Nutrition*.

Rebucci, Alessandro. 2024. "How Effective Were Pandemic Lockdowns?" *Econofact, Public Health*. https://econofact.org/how-effective-were-pandemic-lockdowns

Schreiber, Sarah, and Alexandra Kelly. 2025. "47 Bridal Shower Games and Activities to Keep Your Guests Entertained." marthastewart.com. March 26. https://www.marthastewart.com/7850855/bridal-shower-games-and-activities.

Tully, Tracey. 2020. "Hoping to Buy an Aboveground Pool to Salvage Summer? It May Be Too Late." nytimes.com/2020. June 3. https://www.nytimes.com /2020/06/03/nyregion/coronavirus-above-ground-pools.html.

Wiener-Bronner, Danielle. 2023. "Three Ways Covid Changed the Restaurant Industry." cnn.com/2023. August 14. https://www.cnn.com/2023/08/13 /business/covid-restaurant-industry/index.html.

Adapted from original posting as *ConsumerCorner.2020.Article.03* (https://agribusiness.purdue.edu/consumer_corner/consumer-spending -is-todays-statistic/)

4

SELF-REPORTED 2021 INTENTIONS TO TAKE THE SHOT (OR NOT) BY DEMOGRAPHICS

BY NICOLE J. OLYNK WIDMAR AND COURTNEY BIR

C onsider it March 2021—the one-year mark from which our lives were transformed. Anxiety persists and human lives were lost at rates that have numbed most of us to the realities being faced. In Consumer Corner, we've debated consumer behaviors under duress (recall from *Consumer Corner: Decisions That Shape Supply Chains* by Widmar et al. 2025) and examined how behavioral changes may last longer than we think (in the previous chapter). We've also discussed dairy markets in light of the massive fluctuations of 2020 (Widmar et al., "Much Ado About Dairy?" from *Consumer Corner: Markets We Thought We Knew*, 2025).

In these market conversations, a bright spot emerged in the potential return to some version of normalcy. This hope was anchored in the unprecedented development, manufacturing, and distribution of an FDA-approved vaccine for a virus that had only been acknowledged in a significant and meaningful way a little over a year ago.

In chapter 1 we analyzed COVID-related perceptions and behaviors reported in June 2020. We again collected data in January 2021 from a representative sample of 927 US households to revisit themes of personal and

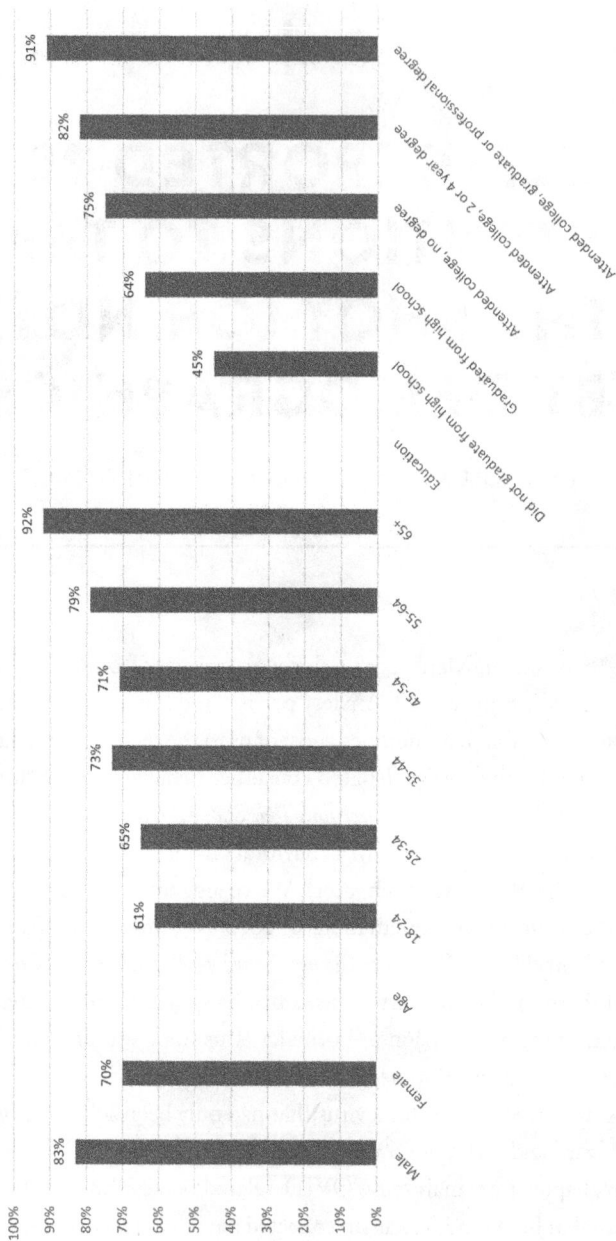

Has or Plans to Obtain Vaccine (n=553)
% of Respondents Within Demographic Categories That Indicate Intention to Get Vaccinated

FIGURE 4.1. Plans to Obtain the COVID-19 Vaccine

societal responsibility, alongside collecting data about individuals' behavior as the pandemic era continued (on and on, so it felt)—this time with vaccines available. That availability marked a major shift from the prior summer, when a vaccine was still an unfulfilled aspiration.

What we learned from our preliminary analyses includes the following:

- 4 percent of respondents reported they had already been fully vaccinated.
- 41 percent of respondents indicated, "I am not yet eligible to obtain the vaccine, but intend to do so once I am eligible."
- 13 percent of respondents responded, "I am eligible to obtain the vaccine and intend to, but have not yet taken steps to do so."
- 24 percent indicated that they do not intend to obtain the vaccine.

We then looked at those who had vaccine intentions by key demographics among those who had been or planned to be vaccinated. In total, more men than women reported vaccine acceptance. We also found that vaccine intentions increase with age and education level.

Vaccines may have been the most powerful tool available to end the pandemic, but personal behaviors such as social distancing and masking still played a huge role in determining the path of the pandemic and the period of recovery.

Adapted from original posting as *ConsumerCorner.2021.Letter.08* (https://agribusiness.purdue.edu/consumer_corner/self-reported-2021 -intentions-to-take-the-shot-or-not-by-demographics/)

5

US ADULTS MOST LIKELY TO WEAR MASKS AND LEAST LIKELY TO REDUCE AROUND-TOWN INTERACTIONS

BY NICOLE J. OLYNK WIDMAR AND COURTNEY BIR

It's still March 2021, and all eyes are on the possibility of an impending recovery from the COVID-19 pandemic. As part of our investigation into personal human behaviors that have impacts on others and on society, we've measured the self-reported likelihood of masking, reducing movement, and social distancing to prevent COVID-19 spread.

In chapter 2, we examined masking behaviors among US residents in June 2020, including regional differences in perceptions. For this new analysis, we collected a nationally representative sample of 927 respondents, all US adults over the age of 18 in January 2021. Given the challenges of achieving the coveted herd immunity—and the then-current lack of an approved vaccine for children—our chapter 4 finding that 24 percent of adults reporting that they do not intend to get vaccinated was troubling. The COVID-19 vaccination may have been the proverbial "light at the end of the tunnel" for some. However, those personal behaviors like social distancing, mask wearing, and reducing interactions with others undoubtedly continued to influence the outcomes of the pandemic. As people grew tired of isolation from family and friends, their willingness to maintain distance decreased.

In our January 2021 survey, the behaviors respondents reported being most likely to engage in from highest to lowest likelihood, were:

1. Wearing a mask or face covering in public
2. Complying with government recommendations regarding social distancing
3. Complying with governmental orders regarding closures or lockdowns
4. Reducing out-of-town travel
5. Reducing the number of nonessential errands/interactions around town

TABLE 5.1. *Propensity to Participate in Behaviors to Mitigate the Spread of COVID-19*

LIKELIHOOD OF PARTICIPATING IN COVID-19 MITIGATION STRATEGIES				
	EXTREMELY UNLIKELY	UNLIKELY	NEUTRAL	LIKELY	EXTREMELY LIKELY
Wear a face mask	5%	3%	10%	13%	69%
Comply with social distancing recommendations	11%	7%	21%	23%	38%
Comply with closures or lockdowns	10%	6%	19%	16%	48%
Reduce travel out of town	6%	6%	17%	17%	53%
Reduce nonessential errands and interactions	6%	4%	13%	19%	58%

The highest mean likelihood for participation was reported for wearing masks. On the positive side, this behavior helped reduce viral spread and facilitated a safer return to schools and other public places. On the negative side, mask wearing has been highly politicized and wasn't adopted quickly or easily by US residents—as we pointed out in chapter 1. Meanwhile, states began rolling back mask requirements just as the federal government reinforced the importance of masking in public transportation and other shared settings. These conflicting policies may have further compounded public confusion.

Conversely, the behavior with the lowest mean likelihood of participation was reducing nonessential errands or interactions around town. Given the duration for which people had been asked to reduce interactions, it was not surprising in their reluctance to stay put.

Even as vaccination campaigns gained speed and record numbers of US adults were vaccinated daily, herd immunity was not in sight. While some adults declined vaccination and children were still ineligible, immunity remained elusive. Thus, while vaccine uptake (discussed in chapter 4) may have dominated headlines, the personal behaviors we'd known about for the better part of a year remained important—despite our collective fatigue.

WORK CITED

Wallheimer, Brian. 2021. "Data Suggest COVID Herd Immunity May Be Hard to Achieve." ag.purdue.edu. March 17. https://ag.purdue.edu/news/2021/03/data-suggest-covid-herd-immunity-may-be-hard-to-achieve.html.

Adapted from original posting as *ConsumerCorner.2021.Letter.10* (https://agribusiness.purdue.edu/consumer_corner/us-adults-most-likely-to-wear-masks-and-least-likely-to-reduce-around-town-interactions/)

6

ONE ECONOMIST'S OVERLY PERSONAL PONDERINGS ON 2020 OFFICE ATTIRE AND RELATED MARKET QUESTIONS

---

t started with a simple, bluntly stated, deep-in-2020 observation: "Whelp, we look awful by any traditional office standard."

I (Nicole) did not decide this on my own—just google "Zoom fashion" or "pandemic fashion." *The New Yorker* even used "slob-chic" in a headline. I didn't invent home workwear, now was I the first to comment on it. But it turns out that I was an A+ participant in the movement.

I suggest we redefine the standards for what "awful" actually means. Ultimately, it's your choice. Redefine what chic is and be done with it. Notably, my answer is *not* that we work to improve our fashion or dressing choices. People are emotionally, physically, and socially fatigued. COVID-fatigue was real—the stress of worrying and being in a constant state of anxiety took a toll, resulting in mental health consequences (COVID-19 Research Working Group 2020). So, as an economist, I ponder the alternatives and consequences (economically and socially) of this change in behavior. I don't suggest I have the right answer on proper procedure or how to determine what will happen in the future.

In a shift from my usual focus on consumption behavior, I've thought about everyday economics since COVID and the allocation of our scarcest resource: time. I have pondered our work-related behaviors given the circumstances, and even though I am probably oversharing a bit for a public forum, I stand by my initial response: I work more when working remotely, partly by repurposing the two hours per day that would have normally been spent getting ready in the morning, getting my kid ready for school (his school was on a laptop for an entire year and pajamas were working just fine), and commuting to and from the Purdue campus.

Everyone's experiences and circumstances are different. Perhaps your everyday work life never changed. Maybe you worked at home for months, balancing work while caring for or schooling children. Perhaps you worked odd hours, trading off responsibilities with other family members to make economic survival possible. Perhaps you were showing up at work and interacting with the public all along in a retail food setting or medical office. Maybe you dealt with the lack of childcare, which was hobbling (okay, destroying) your ability to perform your job. Or you still performed your job while also doing all the childcare and home stuff and wondered how long you could really persist this way.

Even if you weren't personally impacted in your work life, the economy was absolutely impacted. This interconnectedness meant that while your everyday life actions may be the same, society was not (and still isn't). Suffice to say, we were all uniquely impacted—some facing much more serious consequences than others.

I offer you my semi-informed musings about the work-from-home crowd with questions about how we allocate our resources in our everyday lives. But let's be honest—we didn't exactly project our best selves those days.

Consider it March 2021 again. All right, Zoombies—the gig is up. You look awful. And I am judging you with cat hair on my pants and a stain of unknown origin on my shirt. My kid wiped something (food item, I'm choosing to believe) on me earlier, and it's still there. Once upon a time we worried about accessories. Now the bar is cleared if we're even wearing pants. When is the last time you saw a zipper, let alone used one? We've come (or fallen?) a long way in the work-from-home life. We had an entire revolution in retail with respect to clothing, accessories, and especially formal wear. Truth be told, the massive reshaping of retail stores was underway in the United States long before COVID-19 hit, but we certainly accelerated it.

Lessened concern with appearances makes sense in light of the weight of an anxiety-inducing health pandemic and economic crisis on people's minds. How long have you gone without a haircut? That look is now socially expected, maybe even preferred in some circles. When your daily "care capacity" is limited, appearance naturally takes a back seat to caring for children, paying bills, maintaining productivity in your employment, and navigating an entirely new world—often with shattered support systems. This realization brings to light the question of what the long-term expectations for appearances will be. Did our new casual (like, really casual) approach become the new norm? Society has slowly gotten more casual over time anyway, with many office settings adopting more casual attire than the once-expected suits and ties. We wondered if people would even return to wearing pants. A silly thing to ponder but an interesting question that impacted a large variety of markets from clothing and accessories to personal grooming to basically all of retail in one way or another.

Time and space were redefined over the course of the pandemic. I was benefiting from a fluid workday schedule; however, the lack of a daily commute (with my child, aka coworker) actually afforded me increased flexibility to get early morning work done, which is my preferred working time. That aspect was personally helpful, although I acknowledge I was a homebody beforehand and have always preferred my home office for writing compared to any other space. Others struggled with this aspect significantly. Those who work best in offices or coffee shops struggled for months (as did the offices and coffee shops in many cases).

Maybe it was time to redefine *professional*. We were at home more, juggling work, housework, and childcare, perhaps working longer hours to make up for lack of efficiency and interruptions. Yes, there were very obvious mental health costs. Long hours, unclear boundaries, and sustained uncertainty are draining. I'm not an expert in that realm, but I do know that change is hard, and the situation was harder. Together, it was just plain painful, and that is not even accounting for the direct impacts like loss of employment or health.

I've only scratched a tiny piece of the surface, but the cascading effects of the above-mentioned transformations were massive.

Long-term vacation rentals increased in popularity as socially distanced getaways became increasingly popular (Ward 2020). But once physical location wasn't binding, we began to see discussion of working from somewhere else (Hunter 2020). Some who took it to an extreme moved to Barbados for a full year to work remotely. In a press release sent to *BusinessInsider*, the chair of Barbados Tourism Marketing Inc., Sunil Chatrani, invited remote workers by touting the productive potential of Barbados' fiber internet and mobile services, in addition to the ample office real estate offerings (Hoeller 2020). Now, what are the economic implications of this kind of mobility? For starters, there were a variety of questions at the time and amassing press about a potential migration out of expensive cities if residents were no longer tethered geographically, but that is a *much* bigger question, with even more economic layers ... so we'll stop here.

WORKS CITED

COVID-19 Research Working Group. 2020. "'COVID Fatigue' Is Hitting Hard. Fighting It Is Hard, Too, Says UC Davis Health Psychologist." covid19research .ucdavis.edu. July 7. https://covid19research.ucdavis.edu/news/covid-fatigue -hitting-hard-fighting-it-hard-too-says-uc-davis-health-psychologist.

Hoeller, Sophie-Clare. 2020. "Barbados Is Officially Letting People Move There to Work Remotely for a Year, and All You Need to Do Is Fill Out an Application." businessinsider.com. July 23. https://www.businessinsider.com/work -remote-live-caribbean-barbados-new-visa-2020-7#:~:text=Barbados%20has

%20officially%20launched%20its,passport%20and%20birth%20certificate%2C%20electronically.

Hunter, Marnie. 2020. "Working from a Vacation Rental Home? Here's What You Need to Know." cnn.com/travel. June 26. https://www.cnn.com/travel/article/vacation-rental-houses-for-work-pandemic/index.html.

Ward, Terry. 2020. "Vacation Home Rentals Are Hot, Physically Distant Getaways." aarp.org/travel. June 25. https://www.aarp.org/travel/travel-tips/lodging/vacation-rental-social-distance-getaways/.

Adapted from original posting as *ConsumerCorner.2020.Letter.17* (https://agribusiness.purdue.edu/consumer_corner/personal-ponderings-on-2020-office-attire/)

7

COVID-INDUCED LIFESTYLE ADAPTATIONS WE'RE KEEPING

BY NICOLE J. OLYNK WIDMAR AND TORRIE SHERIDAN

---

t's still 2021, and we've learned a lot about pandemic-era adjustments at this point. All right, we get it—2020 was not amazing, and while 2021 isn't quite as toilet paper–focused, it isn't exactly coming up roses just yet for those of us impatiently waiting to access a vaccine and a daily lifestyle more familiar to what we'd been accustomed to a year ago. Mind you, we're not complaining; we're simply frustrated—but pleasant—while donning our Zoom appropriate nonoffice wear (recall from chapter 6), "slob-chic" indeed, and pondering what markets for consumer goods and travel might look like in the "new normal" era (recall from chapter 3).

Over the last twelve months, things in the Purdue University Center for Food and Agricultural Business have been different, just as they have everywhere else. Our once bustling classrooms filled with learning, handshakes, and networking professionals now sit empty most of the time. Instead, Zoom classrooms and virtual networking took over. We adjusted and adapted to the current environment. And while the new heavily online professional development delivery style is different from traditional in-person programming, it's not all bad.

For example, the ability to "wake up" the front row of your classroom is extended to the whole Zoom room, as everyone now has a front-row seat to the arm-waving, impassioned market insights of Dr. Michael Boehlje. And Dr. Dave Downey will cause you to reflect on your value proposition and how to communicate it, regardless of whether he's in the classroom with you or coming to you live on the big screen.

With the many changes and transitions we all faced in our personal and professional lives, we asked Dr. Downey and Dr. Boehlje to reflect on their learnings and analyze positives, in their opinion, that have come from these shifts.

Dr. Downey says that the Center for Food and Agricultural Business (much like everyone else) had a short window of opportunity to differentiate itself. The center was able to quickly adapt to continue providing first-class educational opportunities and has experienced a great deal of positive improvements as a result.

For example, Dr. Downey feels that the opportunity to observe and coach participant learning through virtual breakout rooms has been an instrumental tool. And while we knew body language and listening were important before the pandemic, our increased use of virtual platforms has greatly amplified this importance. We've learned to listen more intently, observe others' body language, become more aware of our own body language, and hone our communication skills. We've also learned that careful integration of visual media into verbal presentations is a necessity for greater effectiveness.

Dr. Boehlje has also learned a thing or two through the center's transitions during the pandemic year, such as how easy it is for participants to zone out during virtual meetings or programs. To reduce this problem, he's found that asking participants to keep their video on increases engagement and interaction. He's also found that building time into the agenda for participant introductions has led to positive impacts on peer-to-peer learning, more effective group discussions, and increased teamwork and engagement.

If you've ever taken a course or participated in a program with Dr. Boehlje, you've likely heard him say "Write it down!" and you're surely familiar with his animated body language and expressions when discussing topics of interest. Dr. Boehlje feels that in virtual settings, writing down instructions and strong organization are even more critical for retention. Additionally, he feels that passion and expression through both verbal and physical cues have an increased role in a virtual environment. As we work to examine others' body language and social cues, it's essential for us to better project ourselves, too.

And while background cues and body language are key players, Dr. Boehlje says content is key. No matter how good you look or how interesting your background may be, it's easy to lose the interest of others in a virtual setting if the content isn't relevant and engaging.

Additionally, both Drs. Downey and Boehlje say that the ability to break down professional development programs into shorter segments using a wider range of channels, such as live sessions and prerecorded videos, has had a positive impact on participant experience. Each channel of delivery can be tailored to unique audiences, and participants have the opportunity to consume content in a manner that fits their learning style.

There are aspects of COVID-era work life that some of us, even the skeptics such as myself (Nicole), have had our eyes opened to. I've learned that sharing a screen with carefully curated materials is more effective at teaching some analytics processes because everyone has a first-class seat in relation to the screen and can easily follow along. I've also learned that my materials must be *more* carefully planned and *much more* carefully curated in advance; I'm now competing for attention in a way that I never was before.

With respect to teaching, recording my own lectures is simpler online and allows attendees to revisit material as many times as they want. This process has caused me to stop and think, "Why wasn't I doing this before?" I plan to continue recording my lectures and posting them for students to review as many times as they wish in the future.

A new generation of learners who have had access to new electronic resources and experience working with virtual teams has come along, and we have had to prepare ourselves for the considerably higher expectations they will have of instructors and facilitators.

Were there any processes you started during the pandemic that caused you to stop and ask yourself, "Why wasn't I doing this before?" Although many of us find ourselves hoping we can return to the old ways of doing things, what we're more likely to experience is the adapted "new normal." And in this new normal, aspects of the pandemic-era life that you actually came to enjoy were sure to be included. A previous study by McKinsey found that even after the pandemic recedes, consumer behaviors such as e-grocery shopping, home nesting (spending on home gyms, renovations, and gardens) and virtual health care are likely to stick around (McKinsey Global Institute 2021).

NICOLE'S ADAPTED "NEW NORMAL"

- More highly integrated home and work lives
- Staying home more, when it works for me and for my work; I like it at home
- Hybrid online and physical professional presence
- Improved accessibility through virtual participation
- Kindergartner FaceTimes grandparents regularly as second nature now
- Lecture/program materials recorded and accessible on demand
- Grocery curbside pickup

TORRIE'S ADAPTED "NEW NORMAL"

- Increased acceptance of working from home
- Spending more time with dogs
- Grocery and shopping curbside pickups
- More cooking at home vs. eating out
- Shopping at and supporting local businesses
- Using Zoom or Microsoft Teams for quick meetings or questions vs. phone calls

DR. DOWNEY'S ADAPTED "NEW NORMAL"

- Spending more physical time with close family
- Using virtual platforms to connect with extended family and friends
- Using virtual breakout rooms during meetings and programs
- Integrating visual experiences into verbal presentations for greater effectiveness

- Utilizing a wider range of communication channels
- Breaking down long programs or learning sessions into shorter segments

DR. BOEHLJE'S "NEW NORMAL"

- Shopping online but still visiting stores for entertainment purposes
- Listening carefully and observing body language
- Using modularization to break up programs and sessions
- Being more intentional about content and organization
- Utilizing different activities to enhance learning success

Straddling the line between work and home life—and working from home with a kid underfoot—isn't exactly easy. However, I (Nicole) have personally appreciated the increased flexibility to work at home with a sick kid rather than missing professional meetings for a kid's sick day. Accessibility to work events online has improved significantly, allowing caretaking responsibilities to coexist with professional responsibilities for many people. This accessibility and opportunity to attend meetings I would have otherwise had to miss has been a nice change. I tend to like being at home more than most, so that part is okay. At the same time, I think I'm ready to travel again—maybe a little absence from this house once in a while would actually help the heart grow fonder?

What are some adaptations from your work and home life that you kept post-pandemic? On the flip side, what are some adaptations that you have come to loathe and are either glad they're gone or wish they'd disappear within your (current) new normal?

WORKS CITED

McKinsey Global Institute. 2021. "The Consumer Demand Recovery and Lasting Effects of COVID-19." mckinsey.com/industries. March 17. https://www.mckinsey.com/industries/consumer-packaged-goods/our-insights/the-consumer-demand-recovery-and-lasting-effects-of-covid-19.

Widmar, Nicole J. Olynk, Michael L. Smith, and Erin Robinson. 2025. *Consumer Corner: Non-Traditional Takes on Consumer-Driven Insights: Decidedly Non-Traditional Insights into Decision Making and Management.* Purdue University Press.

Adapted from original posting as *ConsumerCorner.2021.Letter.11* (https://agribusiness.purdue.edu/consumer_corner/covid-induced -lifestyle-adaptations-post-pandemic/)

8

THE COVID-19 VACCINE EDITION OF PURDUE PETE VERSUS PISTOL PETE

BY NICOLE J. OLYNK WIDMAR AND COURTNEY BIR

I n chapter 2, we reported on the mask-wearing beliefs and intentions of residents of two regions: Purdue University and surrounding states and Oklahoma State University and surrounding states, compared to the rest of the United States. Six months later, in January 2021, we collected new data on personal behaviors associated with COVID-19 spread as well as personal and societal risk factors.

The sample was split into four subgroups: Indiana and surrounding states vs. all others, and Oklahoma and surrounding states vs. all others. We provide a list of states classified in each regional grouping, the Indiana region (comprised of Indiana, Michigan, Ohio, Kentucky, and Illinois), and the Oklahoma region (comprised of Oklahoma, Kansas, Missouri, Arkansas, Texas, New Mexico, and Colorado).

Demographics for the four subsamples of interest are displayed in Table 8.1. Overall, the respondent pool represented the broader US population reasonably well. There were no statistically significant differences between Indiana and the surrounding states and the rest of the United States. For Oklahoma and the surrounding states, only two categories

TABLE 8.1. *Demographics for Oklahoma Region and the Rest of the Country*

	INDIANA + SURROUNDING STATES (N = 136)	NON-INDIANA + SURROUNDING STATES (N = 793)	OKLAHOMA + SURROUNDING STATES (N = 146)	NON-OKLAHOMA + SURROUNDING STATES (N = 783)
Gender				
Male	50	46	49	46
Female	50	54	51	54
Age				
18–24	4	9	10	8
25–34	9	14	15	13
35–44	20	19	27*	18*
45–54	18	16	12	17
55–64	26	19	16	20
65+	23	23	19	24
Income				
$0–$24,999	18	20	20	19
$25,000–$49,999	20	22	18	22
$50,000–$74,999	17	16	16	17
$75,000–$99,999	12	13	21*	11*
$100,000 and higher	33	29	24	31

Education

Education				
Did not graduate from high school	4	2	1	2
Graduated from high school, Did not attend college	23	28	27	27
Attended college, No degree earned	20	22	21	22
Attended college, Associate's or bachelor's degree earned	39	33	38	34
Attended college, Graduate or professional degree earned	14	15	12	16

---

*Indicates the percentage of respondents from that category from Oklahoma and the surrounding states is statistically different from the rest of the country at the < 0.05 level.

Note: There were no statistically significant differences between Indiana and the surrounding states sample and the non-Indiana and the surrounding states sample.

differed statistically significantly from the rest of the United States: the 35–44 age group and the $75,000–$99,000 annual household income bracket.

While masking was promoted to reduce virus transmission, it was ultimately the vaccine that enabled society to begin lifting restrictions. Table 8.2 presents the likelihood of individuals engaging in personal behaviors aimed at preventing the spread of COVID-19 in the nine months following January 2021. Across all four subsamples of US respondents, wearing a mask remained the most likely behavior. Similarly, respondents were least likely to reduce local errands or interactions, regardless of their region.

TABLE 8.2. *Likelihood of Participating in COVID-19 Preventive Behaviors in the 9 Months Following January 2021 (1 = extremely unlikely, 5 = extremely likely)*

	IN STATES	NON-IN STATES	OK STATES	NON-OK STATES
Wear a mask or face covering in public	4.456a $n = 136$	4.372a $n = 792$	4.425a[*] $n = 146$	4.377a[†] $n = 782$
Reduce number of nonessential errands/ interactions around town	3.647b $n = 136$	3.708b $n = 792$	3.692b $n = 146$	3.701b $n = 782$
Reduce out-of-town travel	3.743b $n = 136$	3.885c $n = 792$	3.917bc $n = 145$	3.854c $n = 782$
Comply with government orders regarding closures or lockdowns	4.140c $n = 136$	4.033d $n = 791$	4.062c $n = 145$	4.046d $n = 782$
Comply with government recommendations regarding social distancing	4.222ac $n = 135$	4.187e $n = 792$	4.199ac $n = 146$	4.191e $n = 781$

[*] Matching letters down a column indicate the means are not statistically different at the 0.05 level. For example, the mean for wear a mask or face covering in public is not statistically different from comply with government recommendations regarding social distancing for Oklahoma and the surrounding states. Differing letters indicate the means are statistically different at the 0.05 level. For example, the mean for wear a mask or face covering in public is statistically different from reduce number of nonessential errands/interactions around town for Oklahoma and the surrounding states.

[†] The mean responses for each personal behavior are not statistically different between those in Oklahoma and the surrounding states and the rest of the United States.

TABLE 8.3. *Vaccine Intention, Percentage of Respondents*

	OKLAHOMA AND SURROUNDING STATES	NON-OKLAHOMA	INDIANA AND SURROUNDING STATES	NON-INDIANA
Have already received two doses of the vaccine	8%	3%	3%	4%
Have obtained the first dose of the vaccine and intend to obtain the second	8%	6%	7%	6%
Have obtained the first dose of the vaccine and do not intend to obtain the second	2%	3%	2%	3%
Have scheduled for the first dose of the vaccine	6%	5%	4%	5%
Currently eligible and intend to obtain the vaccine but no current plans	12%	12%	12%	13%
Not yet eligible to obtain the vaccine	36%	41%	44%	40%
No intention to obtain the vaccine	19%	25%	24%	24%
Other	9%	5%	4%	5%

Note: No statistical differences were observed between Indiana and the surrounding states and the rest of the United States, or between Oklahoma and the surrounding states and Indiana and the surrounding states.

At the time of data collection in January 2021, the availability of a vaccine was still limited across much of the United States. Yet, a patchwork of availability existed with some states and regions experiencing much more availability than others and with highly variable requirements and rollout plans being exercised. Respondents were asked about their vaccination status, ranging from having been fully vaccinated to not intending to be vaccinated, even once it became available to them. Table 8.3 displays vaccination intentions by US adults in the four regions of the United States defined. In total, 19 percent of respondents in Oklahoma and surrounding states did not plan to get vaccinated, whereas 24–25 percent of respondents said the same in the other three regions of interest.

While people showed strong intentions to continue masking, they were not as willing to reduce interactions or travel. Vaccine intentions were concerning, with 19–25 percent of respondents across studied regions who did not intend to be vaccinated. Likely, given the timing of data collection, those who reported having been vaccinated was more a reflection of vaccine availability in their state than anything else measurable. Individuals eventually had the opportunity to take their stated intentions and make them reality. Given the wide interest in returning to normal, stopping societal spread of COVID-19 was imperative. Personal behaviors, including practices such as mask wearing and social distancing, alongside vaccination of eligible adults, were thought to help bring the pandemic era to an end. Understanding regional behavioral intentions can inform both public policy and the development of educational campaigns aimed at informing the general public, which helped support the "return to normal" we all were seeking.

———————

Adapted from original posting as *ConsumerCorner.Article.04* (https://agribusiness.purdue.edu/consumer_corner/purdue-pete-and -pistol-pete-covid-19-vaccine-edition/)

9

SOCIETAL VALUES AND PERSONAL RISKY BEHAVIORS REMAIN FOR SIX MONTHS IN A PANDEMIC ERA—EXCEPT WE'RE DRINKING MORE ALCOHOL

BY NICOLE J. OLYNK WIDMAR AND COURTNEY BIR

After our previous analyses of mask-wearing behavior to prevent the spread of COVID-19 (chapter 1), we turned our attention to how individuals perceive personal versus societal responsibilities. By the summer of 2020, media coverage of mask wearing (or more often, the refusal to wear masks) began focusing heavily on the political polarization surrounding this public health issue.

An article by Jordan Smith, a summer reporter for *The Exponent*, interviewed me (Nicole) for a story titled "Majority Says Masks Curb Disease, but Wearing Habits Vary." In that article Smith wrote:

Mere science won't convince everyone, Widmar notes. The story references President Donald Trump's avid refusal to wear a mask for the beginning months of the pandemic. Myths abound about the effectiveness of the anti-malarial medication hydroxychloroquine and the severity of symptoms from which COVID-19 patients suffer.

Widmar could not definitively state whether residents of Indiana, a reliably conservative state, are segmented by political parties in their beliefs about the coronavirus. Her survey did not explicitly track political affiliation, but instead offered statements about societal values to detect political trends.

"Agreement with the statement 'gun ownership is a right based on the US Constitution' was negatively correlated with the belief masks had a role in society related to the spread of COVID-19," the study finds, meaning that agreeing with the first statement is associated with disagreement that masks play a role. "Agreement with the statements 'Health care is a human right', and 'I always wear my seat belt when driving' were positively correlated with the belief masks had a role in society."

You may recall, we collected data in January 2021 to find out more about societal values, as well as their engagement in personal behaviors associated with risk, such as smoking, drinking alcohol, and seatbelt use. We then compared these results to our June 2020 data. Among the personal behavior statements, the highest level of agreement across both time periods was that respondents agree they always wear a seatbelt when driving. Societally, respondents in both time periods believe we have a responsibility to protect the elderly and children, although there is less agreement that health care is a human right.

Interestingly, the mean agreement levels for almost all of the personal risky behaviors and societal value statements remained unchanged in our January 2021 sample compared to the June 2020 sample. The one single exception—the statement "I frequently drink alcohol"—saw a statistically significant increase in agreement from 2.20 to 2.35 on a 5-point scale (1 = strongly disagree; 5 = strongly agree). It's possible that alcohol consumption behaviors changed during the pandemic, or perhaps that

TABLE 9.1. *Levels of Agreement Between Societal Value Statements and Participation in Behaviors Associated with Possible Personal Risk Factors*

	JANUARY 2021 MEAN	JUNE 2020 MEAN
I am in the higher risk group for complications of COVID-19	2.8	2.86
Someone in my household is in the higher risk group for complications of COVID-19	2.94	2.92
I believe we have the social responsibility to protect the elderly	4.27	4.25
I believe we have the social responsibility to protect children	4.36	4.37
I frequently smoke	1.88	1.95
I frequently drink alcohol	2.35	2.2
I always wear my seatbelt when driving	4.53	4.49
Health care is a human right	4.07	4.01
Gun ownership is a right based on the US Constitution	3.83	3.78

willingness to self-report frequent drinking changed while actual behaviors did not. Regardless, the finding merits attention: In a period marked by high stress and disrupted routines, this behavior shift could have public health implications.

———————

Adapted from original posting as *ConsumerCorner.2021.Letter.12* (https://agribusiness.purdue.edu/consumer_corner/societal-values-and -personal-risky-behaviors-unchanged-during-pandemic/)

10

WE'RE TALKING ABOUT TOILET PAPER AND MEAT AGAIN

NICOLE J. OLYNK WIDMAR AND COURTNEY BIR

B y July 2020, COVID-19 had altered nearly every aspect of daily life. While its impacts were undeniable, they were far from uniform. As the age-old wisdom goes, we might all be in the same storm, but we're not sailing in the same boat. Do you use public transportation to access groceries and essential items? Do you have access to a personal vehicle and a nearby supermarket? And perhaps the most debated conundrum for agriculture and food supply chains: Does your supermarket have the exact items you want to purchase when you want them?

A full-page ad in the Sunday *New York Times* in April 2020, placed by Tyson Foods board chairman John Tyson and titled *The Food Supply Chain Is Breaking,* elicited national concern and widespread media coverage. In response, Tyne Morgan published a follow-up piece called *Is the Food Supply Chain Actually Breaking?*, which featured an interview with Dr. Jayson Lusk:

> "I have a little different view," says Jayson Lusk, a Purdue University agricultural economist. "I think by and large, throughout this crisis, the food supply chain has responded remarkably well. Yes, we had a short period [when] some grocery store shelves were empty, but by and

large, food was available. It might have been a different variety or different brand than you're accustomed to buying. But the foods system responded remarkably well to a completely unexpected and unprecedented event. We certainly have some very serious challenges coming up in the meat sector, but that doesn't mean the entire system is broken." (Morgan 2021)

So, we know what food systems and economics experts had to say. But, what did the US public have to say? We're all impacted heavily by our own echo chambers. Part of understanding our consumers is to free ourselves from our own silos of concern to consider the experiences and perceptions of others. We collected data between June 12 and 20, 2020, about impacts of COVID-19 on US households as part of a study of COVID-19 perceptions with respect to personal values and behaviors associated with reopening. Chapter 1's analysis of behavior and chapter 2's focus on mask usage beliefs both draw from this same dataset.

As part of this research, we measured self-reported household-level impacts of COVID-19 using five impact statements on 1,198 households in a representative sample of the United States. First, we asked respondents to indicate whether each of the five statements applied to them.

Next, those who indicated that the statement applied to them rated the level of impact on a scale from 1 (not impacted) to 5 (impacted). Based on early pandemic experiences, we expected meat, dairy, and perishable foods availability to be among the top concerns. Surprisingly, it was not. In

TABLE 10.1. *Self-Reported Applicability of COVID-19 Impact Statements*

	YES	NO
Activities related to respondents' work/school	73%	27%
Ability to execute travel plans	78%	22%
Ability to find meat, milk, and perishables at the grocery store	97%	3%
Ability to buy paper products	98%	2%
Respondents' daily activities outside of work/school	92%	8%

TABLE 10.2. *Mean Level of Reported Impact for Respondents for Whom the Following Statements Applied*

Activities related to respondents' work/school	3.50
Ability to execute travel plans	3.89
Ability to find meat, milk, and perishables at the grocery store	3.01
Ability to buy paper products	3.47
Respondents' daily activities outside of work/school	3.56

Note: Impact ranges from 1 to 5.

fact, it ranked fifth (last) among the five statements provided. One could argue, but the fact remains among options presented that the meat and milk category and perishable foods was statistically, and practically, last in self-reported impacts.

In a nutshell: US residents' self-reported data suggests that the availability of perishable groceries (including meat and dairy) was less impacted than paper products, daily activities, travel plans, and school or work activities.

This isn't to say we didn't face supply chain challenges. We did. Shoppers across the country experienced empty shelves. It was a struggle to get fresh dairy products and meat products into supermarkets fast enough to supply the rapid increase in demand of shoppers as they headed home to quarantine for a (then) unspecified amount of time. People went to the supermarket and could *not* get what they wanted. Dairy plants struggled to process the rapidly shifting demand for products for home consumption versus making products for schools and food service. Meat plants shut down as they faced outbreaks among workers, leaving livestock stranded on farms with no processing capabilities to be found elsewhere. These impacts were severe and very real. We do not intend to downplay the very real pain felt by agricultural industries. Meat industries, in particular, suffered significantly to keep up with demand, and there were negative impacts throughout that supply chain at various times.

Knowing what we know now, one may suggest that agricultural and food supply chains need to do some introspective thinking about resiliency versus redundancy. As consumers we are always looking for cheaper items, cheaper choices, and affordable food items. Supply chains are pushed to streamline and optimize for efficiency. But how much resiliency is sacrificed when redundancy is removed in the name of cost savings? Redundancy is not free—it comes with a cost—but it is a good thing too. How much do we value resilience and are we willing to pay for some redundancy in the systems?

With the benefit of time (the insights from this chapter were written in late July 2020), the US food system has proved to be more resilient than it was given credit for in some of the earlier days of the COVID-19 lockdowns. That does not mean there isn't room for improvement by firms involved in the food chain; there is always room for improvement. Many firms have made investments in resiliency already. That also didn't mean there wasn't room for regulation or legislation to force practices and investment to improve resiliency. There were rough days and real moments of uncertainty, like when shoppers couldn't get what they wanted and systems strained to keep up.

While everyone has faced, and may still face, pressure from the COVID-19 economic hangover, the food system in the United States has provided safe and (mostly) plentiful products in locations where it was demanded and at the time it was demanded. At least our data suggests that respondents were reporting relatively less impact from perishable food product availability than from the other statements provided.

WORK CITED

Morgan, Tyne. 2021. "Is the Food Supply Chain Actually Breaking?" *The Scoop.* https://www.thedailyscoop.com/food-supply-chain-actually-breaking

———————

Adapted from original posting as *ConsumerCorner.2020.Letter.13* (https://agribusiness.purdue.edu/consumer_corner/talking-about-toilet -paper-and-meat-again/)

11

REFLECTING ON COVID-19 CONSUMER BEHAVIOR

C onsumer behavior was reshaped multiple times during the COVID-19 pandemic, just as it has been reshaped during past societal crises. For example, you may recall victory gardens (aka war gardens) during World War II or the deeply ingrained thriftiness of those who lived through the Great Depression. These events left lasting marks on how people consumed, saved, and spent. Early in the pandemic, many of us questioned how consumer behavior would change in response to both the health crisis and its ensuing recession long before we realized how long pandemic precautions would remain in place.

In chapter 3, we reflected on the initial wave of consumer behavior changes (like hoarding toilet paper and hand sanitizer) and how those short-term responses receded and have been replaced by long-run changes that have stuck with us (and will for years).

What we call consumer behavior comprises changes in consuming, shopping, saving, reusing, and hoarding. Although, upon reflection, it might be more accurate to relabel these actions as "changes in household economic decision-making" or "changes in home economics," as not all changes involve consumption. In fact, some are quite the opposite of consumption.

Try to recall life in mid-2021. At the time, many in the United States seemed to believe the post-pandemic recovery period had begun. Precautionary practices were being rolled back, and even in the most cautious states, media attention had largely shifted away from overcrowded health care facilities to crowded vacation destinations. Yet in many parts of the world, the acute medical pain of the pandemic was far from over (Duroseau et al. 2023). And globally, the long-term market adjustments and the potentially generation-long human behavioral shifts were only just beginning to unfold. By late 2023, the United States saw considerable price inflation driven by activity in food markets, energy markets, and supply chain issues (Bernanke and Blanchard 2023). While some of the inflation was fueled by other global events—such as Russia's invasion of Ukraine and recurring outbreaks of avian flu—these secondary drivers piled onto the inflationary spike that many central bankers failed to anticipate (Bernanke and Blanchard 2023).

Regardless of how one viewed the likely path to recovery, changes in how we behave as individuals (how we shop, work, care for our families, and manage our money) have and will undoubtedly continue to exist. We are all products of our collective experiences, and we're riddled with biases, fears, and other problematic characteristics that regularly wreak havoc on our decision-making. The experiences of the COVID-19 pandemic and its economic instability aftermath will continue to shape behaviors of individuals, households, societies, and economies.

While all eyes (and most news outlets) are fixated on markets during crises, human behavior—how people react—is often underappreciated. How do people shop after they've experienced a forcible shift to online shopping during the pandemic? How do parents juggle work and childcare after living through a period when both felt impossible to manage at once? Consumers' behavior and how they manage household economics is often more complicated, especially memory shaped by oversized, disruptive events. Behavioral changes following crises can be remarkably persistent (and as earlier stated, underappreciated).

No doubt, the immediate impacts of the pandemic, followed by waves of recovery, lasted longer than most could have possibly anticipated or imagined back in February 2020. While *Consumer Corner* has touched on many topics, COVID-19 has been an indelible part of the series. Consumer behavior during COVID-19 may have been unique in many ways (yes, we're still talking about toilet paper), but the broader pattern of decision-making in response to external forces beyond our control are universal and enduring. Understanding how individuals adapt when forced to react to situations or disruptions—whether brought on by nature, markets, other people—is critical. And the lessons we take from COVID-19 may help us better navigate the next crisis.

WORKS CITED

Bernanke, Ben, and Olivier Blanchard. 2023. *What Caused the U.S. Pandemic-Era Inflation?* Hutchins Center on Fiscal and Monetary Policy at the Brookings Institution.

Duroseau, Brenice, Nodar Kipshidze, and Rupali Jayant Limaye. 2023. "The Impact of Delayed Access to COVID-19 Vaccines in Low- and Lower-Middle-Income Countries." *Frontiers in Public Health.*

Adapted from original posting as *ConsumerCorner.2021.Letter.24* (https://agribusiness.purdue.edu/consumer_corner/covid-19-consumer-behavior-contributions-june-2020-july-2021/)

12

CONSUMER CORNER READERS WEIGHED IN ON PANDEMIC-INDUCED LIFESTYLE ADAPTATIONS

The world after the COVID-19 pandemic is not the same as the world before it. In our efforts to cultivate a "new normal" by mid-2021 (and thereafter), we have all engaged in some variation of kicking, screaming, and mourning of the loss of the old days. As humans, we are generally resistant to change, and the roller coaster of adjustments left emotional and psychological marks. While we're not exactly fans of change either here at Consumer Corner, we've attempted to find the silver lining in skills we developed or new ways of doing things we have come to enjoy. Basically, we are attempting to grow from our experiences, even if we would not have chosen these experiences if we had the option.

In chapter 7, we visited with Drs. Downey and Boehlje about the adaptations they've decided to keep (by choice) and shared some of our own. We even shared professional adaptations within the Center for Food and

Agricultural Business and in the classroom, inviting feedback from stakeholders to help us continue refining our processes (Sheridan 2021).

We also asked you—our loyal Consumer Corner readers—to weigh in on pandemic-induced adaptations that you will and won't keep going forward. Table 12.1 shows what we heard from the $n = 25$ of you who partook in our survey (we've summarized the data collected as of the end of June 2021).

On the personal front, a few themes stood out. Collectively, we love online shopping, and almost all of us are fond of online grocery shopping with curbside pickup or delivery. Always being at home resonates with some of us, although certainly not all. And, for the most part, a lot of us strongly dislike a lack of personal travel. However, not everyone agrees (probably all of the hardcore homebodies).

WHAT ABOUT WORKING FROM HOME?

The answer is . . . it's complicated. In professional circles, remote work remains hotly debated. Who was called back in? Which companies continued to support remote roles? Among our small sampling of respondents, working from home received a strong thumbs-up.

Switching gears to the professional or work-related changes, we find consistency in the sense that we like working from home; however, we do not like only seeing colleagues online. Some respondents even appreciated the end of casual "water cooler chats," while a staggering number liked online meetings (and, if you recall from chapter 6, the relaxed dress code that comes with them). Interestingly, our opinions split when it came to work-related travel. Notably, as a group, we missed personal travel but are much less nostalgic for work-type travel. Taken together, respondents liked online meetings and loved working from home while simultaneously being unhappy with only seeing our colleagues online. Lastly, some respondents reported not being thrilled at the blurring of work and home lines. It's clear that navigating hybrid expectations— "always on" online and increasingly "back in person" was a tricky balancing act for many.

TABLE 12.1. *Lifestyle Changes at Home That We Love or Want to Leave Behind*

	ONLINE SHOPPING FOR ALMOST EVERYTHING	LESS PERSONAL TRAVEL	WORKING FROM HOME	DELIVERY & CURBSIDE PICKUP	ONLINE GROCERY SHOPPING	I AM ALWAYS AT HOME
I strongly like this change	76%	12%	76%	54%	36%	61%
I don't care much about this	24%	20%	16%	38%	45%	17%
I strongly dislike this change	0%	68%	4%	4%	9%	17%
This does not apply to me	0%	0%	4%	4%	9%	4%

Note: Table shows % of respondents who chose each option.

TABLE 12.2. *Lifestyle Changes at Work That We Love or Want to Leave Behind*

	ONLINE MEETINGS	LESS WORK TRAVEL	WORK FROM HOME	HOME AND WORK LIVES ARE BLURRING	ONLY SEE COLLEAGUES ONLINE	NO "WATER COOLER" TALK
I strongly like this change	80%	42%	83%	28%	15%	23%
I don't care much about this	12%	25%	13%	56%	30%	42%
I strongly dislike this change	8%	25%	0%	16%	56%	27%
This does not apply to me	0%	8%	4%	0%	0%	8%

Note: Table shows % of respondents who chose each option.

These findings also suggest there's fertile ground for future research (note to self!). How do work-from-home preferences vary on whether someone is managing caretaking responsibilities alongside professional ones? Do attitudes vary regionally, according to career stage, or stage of life? These are all interesting empirical questions.

WORK CITED

Sheridan, T. (2021, May 3). *Practicing What We Preach: Inviting Feedback on Our COVID-Induced Adaptations.* Retrieved from agribusiness.purdue.edu /consumer_corner: https://agribusiness.purdue.edu/consumer_corner /practicing-what-we-preach/.

Adapted from original posting as *ConsumerCorner.2021.Letter.26* (https://agribusiness.purdue.edu/consumer_corner/you-weighed-in-on -pandemic-induced-lifestyle-adaptations-heres-what-you-said/)

13

ALTRUISM, FREE RIDING, SOCIAL PRESSURE, AND WILLFUL NONCOMPLIANCE

BASED UPON AND INSPIRED BY BIR AND WIDMAR (2021).

W e know that human behaviors shape the course of pandemics (and will influence pandemic recovery as well). It is the cumulative impact of millions of individual decisions and behaviors that ultimately determine the course of pandemics and disease spread within populations. But human decision-making and behavior are complicated. Fatigue sets in on top of continuous confusion and motivations vary widely.

Possibilities for free riding, altruism, peer pressure (i.e., bandwagoning behavior), and protest or angry resistance regarding mask-wearing behaviors in the United States were recognized by late 2020 and early 2021.

Free riding is fundamentally taking advantage of the efforts of others to establish some collective good without actually contributing oneself. Free riding is commonly talked about in the context of vaccination decisions, but it applies in a number of other public health behaviors and outcomes.

Bandwagoning behavior reflects actions or activities that are currently fashionable or socially supported, often recognized as peer pressure or coming from some amount of societal inertia.

Altruism is a selfless concern for others or generally caregiving for others beyond oneself.

In our research, we hypothesized that mask compliance was related to personal beliefs about public health, along with demographic factors. We found that people who believed that wearing masks protected others were more likely to report voluntarily wearing them, providing possible evidence of altruism. Perceiving social pressure negatively impacted the probability of voluntary mask wearing among those who believed masks have a role in society, suggesting social shaming won't increase compliance. And free riding was one possible explanation for why individuals may self-report that masks have a role in society but simultaneously self-report not wearing one. Behavior possibly attributed to free riding, but also to incomplete knowledge, confusion, and pandemic fatigue.

The COVID-19 pandemic offered a relevant example and real-time context for exploring these individual behaviors that have societal impacts, but the concepts are far from new. Vaccination decisions—such as annual flu shots—are commonly framed around both personal and community protection. Shared experiences may aid in understanding why some societies are more compliant with public health protective measures than others, specifically those nations lacking firsthand experience with dire public health consequences. Those nations may be less likely to take up mandates than countries in which significant public health events are in recent memory. But the social and societal memory argument is far from simple. We found that perceiving personal social pressure negatively impacted the probability of voluntary mask wearing, even among those who self-stated masks have a role in society. Thus, while societal memory may matter, our findings suggest social shaming won't change the circumstances and convince individuals to wear a mask in public.

In contrast to vaccinations, which are not visibly apparent in daily interactions, mask-wearing (or the lack thereof) in public is immediately observable. Handwashing after using a restroom, by contrast, falls somewhere in between—it's visible, but only in specific settings. We all know we are supposed to wash our hands, but we've also seen the statistics to know that many (far too many) people don't. We've known our whole lives that we should wash our hands after using the restroom (especially a public restroom!). In that light, the notion that people would universally "just wear a mask" was never that simple. The bottom line? In a society where we struggle to achieve universal handwashing, it's not that surprising that widespread public mask usage proved difficult to achieve.

WORK CITED

Bir, C., and N. J. Widmar. 2021. "Social Pressure, Altruism, Free-Riding, and Non-Compliance in Mask Wearing by US Residents in Response to COVID-19 Pandemic." *Social Sciences & Humanities Open.*

_____

Adapted from original posting as *ConsumerCorner.2021.Letter.40* (https://agribusiness.purdue.edu/consumer_corner/altruism-free-riding -social-pressure-and-willful-non-compliance/)

14

US MEAT MARKET PERFORMANCE DURING THE COVID-19 ERA

U S meat markets got quite the spotlight during the pandemic era. A full-page ad in the Sunday *New York Times* by Tyson Foods board chairman John Tyson in April 2020 entitled, "The Food Supply Chain Is Breaking" elicited national concern and corresponding media response (Gibson 2020). In response, journalist Tyne Morgan interviewed agricultural economist Dr. Jayson Lusk and followed up with a piece aptly entitled, "Is the Food Supply Chain Actually Breaking?" (Morgan 2021).

> "I have a little different view," says Jayson Lusk, a Purdue University agricultural economist. "I think by and large, throughout this crisis, the food supply chain has responded remarkably well. Yes, we had a short period where some grocery store shelves were empty, but by and large, food was available. It might have been a different variety or different brand than you're accustomed to buying. But the foods system responded remarkably well to a completely unexpected and unprecedented event.

We certainly have some very serious challenges coming up in the meat sector, but that doesn't mean the entire system is broken."

This debate inspired a research project dedicated to US meat market functionality during 2019 and 2020 focused on understanding both the media attention and the realities. The result was a peer-reviewed publication in *Meat Science* titled, "Perception Versus Reality of the COVID-19 Pandemic in U.S. Meat Markets" (Widmar et al. 2022).

This paper confirmed that meat production in the United States declined in the spring of 2020 during the pandemic (Widmar et al. 2022). The total meat production in April and May 2020 was 1.5 billion pounds—about 10 percent less than in the same time period in 2019. While there was an uptick in total media mentions about meat during this time period, it was nowhere near as high a spike as we saw in the chicken sandwich wars of August 2019 or even Thanksgiving 2019 (Widmar et al. 2022).

But did this cause an actual shortage? No, there wasn't a shortage. "The notable decrease in meat production in April and May 2020 did not yield a shortage in the US marketplace due to the ample stocks of meat in cold storage which were drawn down during this time period of decreased production" (Widmar et al. 2022).

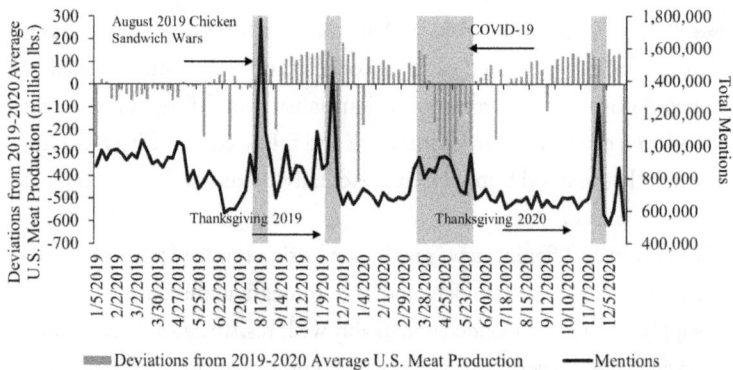

FIGURE 14.1. Timeline Showing the Total Mentions and Deviation from the 2019–2020 Average Meat Production Levels. *Source:* A version of this image appeared as Figure 1 in Widmar et al. (2022).

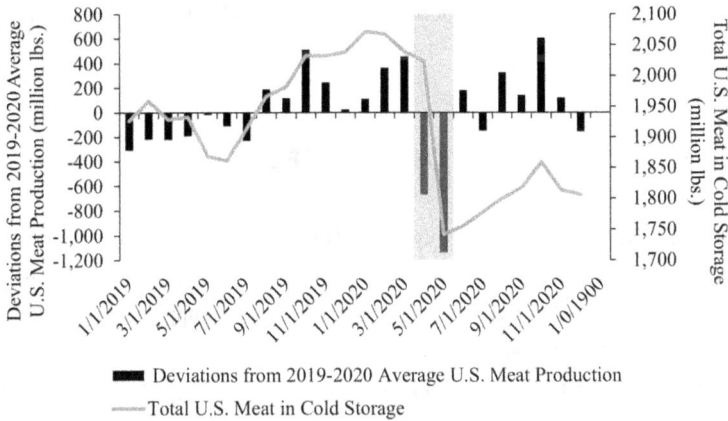

FIGURE 14.2. Deviations in Average Levels of US Meat Production Compared to Total Meat in Cold Storage. *Source:* A version of this image appeared as Figure 3 in Widmar et al. (2022).

While there was a notable fall in meat production in April and May 2020, there was a rebound by the first week of June 2020, drawing down meat in cold storage. Although consumers may have occasionally encountered empty shelves or been unable to find specific cuts of meat on a given day, meat remained broadly available. Net sentiment in online media searches declined notably in the early days of the pandemic, although there were also reactions to non-COVID events uncovered during this time period, and the net sentiment remained positive (24) on the scale of -100 to +100 (Widmar et al. 2022).

Taken together, the authors summarize this by saying, "Despite the ongoing conversations about the pandemic revealing vulnerability in the meat supply chain, a direct comparison between perception and reality reveals that total meat production in the United States showed resiliency and efficient recovery after the April and May 2020 declines due to COVID-19—in this case, perception did reflect reality" (Widmar et al. 2022).

They further note that calls to introduce redundancies in the meat supply chain—via disaggregation or increased reliance on local, direct-to-consumer models—may be intuitively appealing but lack rationale from an efficiency or resiliency standpoint (Hobbs 2021; Ma and Lusk 2021; Lusk et al. 2021).

WORKS CITED

Gibson, Kate. 2020. "'Food Supply Chain Is Breaking,' Tyson Foods Chairman Warns amid Meat Plant Shutdowns." cbsnews.com/news. April 27. https://www.cbsnews.com/news/tyson-foods-chairman-food-supply-chain-breaking-meat-plant-shutdowns-coronavirus-pandemic/.

Hobbs, Jill E. 2021. "The Covid-19 Pandemic and Meat Supply Chains." *Meat Science.*

Lusk, Jayson, Glenn T. Tonsor, and Lee L. Schultz. 2021. "Beef and Pork Marketing Margins and Price Spreads During COVID-19." *Applied Economic Perspectives and Policy.*

Ma, Meilin, and Jayson Lusk. 2021. "Concentration and Resilience in the U.S. Meat Supply Chains." *NBER Working Papers.*

Morgan, Tyne. 2021. "Is the Food Supply Chain Actually Breaking?" porkbusiness.com/news. October 28. https://www.porkbusiness.com/news/industry/food-supply-chain-actually-breaking.

Widmar, Nicole J. Olynk, Nathanael M. Thompson, Courtney Bir, and Eugene Kwaku Mawutor Nuworsu. 2022. "Perception Versus Reality of the COVID-19 Pandemic in U.S. Meat Markets." *Meat Science.*

———

Adapted from original posting as *ConsumerCorner.2022.Letter.15* (https://agribusiness.purdue.edu/consumer_corner/us-meat-market-performance-during-the-covid-19-era/)

15

HOME, OFFICE, BOTH, NEITHER

NICOLE J. OLYNK WIDMAR AND COURTNEY BIR

The pandemic had a profound impact on work environments. As many started working from home, even our office attire began changing. We must admit that "Zoom-chic" fashion left a lot to be desired by pre-pandemic standards. Meetings became more awkward with small talk interrupted by the occasional technical difficulty. Even when restrictions were lifted, work today is in some ways different from pre-COVID work—even for those of us who work in person. We see more advanced digital communication platforms, and companies allowing remote and hybrid work can't get their entire teams in the same room together. The 2019 normal is never coming back, so it's time to confidently embrace the future instead of hoping for a return to the past.

Let's take a moment to revisit a 2020 comment made in chapter 6:

> I was benefiting from a fluid workday schedule; however the lack of a daily commute (with my child, aka coworker) actually afforded me increased flexibility to get early morning work done, which is my preferred working time. That aspect was personally helpful, although I acknowledge I was a homebody beforehand and have always preferred my home office for writing compared to any other space. Others struggled with this aspect significantly. Those who work best in offices or

coffee shops struggled for months (as did the offices and coffee shops in many cases).

Flipping ahead to the diary from 2022, we find this update: "Wow, we were naïve thinking about short-term adjustments to workplaces in 2020. Or maybe we were all emotionally maxed out from the juggling act and persistent strain of the unknown at that time. Either way, the changes to downtown locations, office spaces, real estate, and numerous economy sectors of the economy since have been intense and sweeping, and definitely not short-term."

While the term *Great Resignation* was applied to 2021 (Parker and Horowitz 2022), headlines in 2022 continued with, "The Great Resignation Is Still in Full Swing" (Iacurci 2022). Clearly, the shift in how and where we work—and live—evolved and is ongoing. Work-life balance, or perhaps integration, remains a persistent simultaneous discussion.

Opening up our 2022 data, we've sorted responses by whether respondents' jobs could be performed remotely. Response options included: Yes, Sometimes/Partially, or No. Considering these elements associated with time and space, we were interested in what type of spending was taking place on things like commutes, coffee on-the-go, and so on.

Regardless of whether one's work could be done remotely or not, the largest share of respondents across all three categories were spending about the same as before the pandemic. Dare we say this was normal spending? Among those who could work remotely in the fall of 2021, the second most common response was *spending more* than pre-pandemic. In contrast, for those whose jobs could not be performed remotely, the second

TABLE 15.1. *Spending on "To-Go" Beverages*

	REMOTE	HYBRID	ON-SITE
Less	28	25	26
About the Same	69	41	77
More	35	21	23
Not Applicable/Never Spent on this	34	15	41

Note: Figures in the table reflect the count of respondents out of 751.

most common (by a tiny margin) was *spending less*. So, remote workers are more likely to spend the same or more, while in-person workers are more likely to spend the same or less. Really? Not what was expected, but perhaps remote workers are seeking reasons to get out of the house. Or maybe they're craving outings. We can only hypothesize, but when we feel trapped at home, we're all looking for a reason to get out more, even if it isn't to our physical work location.

When it comes to dining in restaurants, most respondents reported spending less or about the same. A higher proportion of respondents who could work from home reported spending more than their counterparts who couldn't work remotely or could do so only partially.

Takeout food followed a similar trend. The most common response across all work categories was spending about the same. The second most common was spending more in fall 2021 than pre-pandemic, regardless of work location. Given the takeout food revolution—and its continued popularity—this increase is unsurprising. The real question may have been, how long will this last?

TABLE 15.2. *Spending at Restaurants While Dining In*

	REMOTE	HYBRID	ON-SITE
Less	62	41	70
About the Same	61	39	75
More	36	13	11
Not Applicable/Never Spent on this	7	9	11

Note: Figures in the table reflect the count of respondents out of 751.

TABLE 15.3. *Spending on "To-Go" Foods*

	REMOTE	HYBRID	ON-SITE
Less	29	22	26
About the Same	77	45	92
More	47	28	35
Not Applicable/Never Spent on this	13	7	14

Note: Figures in the table reflect the count of respondents out of 751.

TABLE 15.4. *Spending on Commuting*

	REMOTE	HYBRID	ON-SITE
Less	44	30	29
About the Same	71	44	94
More	32	21	26
Not Applicable/Never Spent on this	19	7	18

Note: Figures in the table reflect the count of respondents out of 751.

TABLE 15.5. *Spending on Travel*

	REMOTE	HYBRID	ON-SITE
Less	54	44	62
About the Same	61	29	66
More	30	19	9
Not Applicable/Never Spent on this	21	10	30

Note: Figures in the table reflect the count of respondents out of 751.

Unsurprisingly, those who could work remotely saw the most pronounced reduction in commuting expenses. Still, "about the same" remained the most common answer for every category of worker, with spending less a close second, even among those who indicated they could not work from home. Also notable: A not-insignificant proportion of respondents indicated that they were spending more on commuting in the fall of 2021 than pre-pandemic. While we were unable to tease out why, some respondents may have taken new jobs during this time or moved, leading to now higher commuting expenses as people return to physical work locations. This data was collected before the recent rise in gas prices, but perhaps commuting costs rose when markets for cars tightened and other tightened supply chains factors took hold.

Travel spending is a particularly interesting expenditure to analyze, which received a great deal of press and media attention throughout the pandemic. The most popular answer for those who worked remotely and those who couldn't was to spend about the same in fall 2021 as they did pre-pandemic. In contrast, those who could work remotely sometimes or partially more often reported spending less. It's hard to know whether these differences are truly tied to work modality, although it cannot be ruled out that a person's ability to work from anywhere affects their willingness or ability to travel (and thus their total travel expenditure).

We are confident in saying that the past several years revealed that, as a collective society, we did not simply work from home for a bit and then return to our pre-2020 behaviors. Instead, we navigated a more complex negotiation around work-life balance (or perhaps integration) that is far more holistic than we might have naively imagined at the start.

WORKS CITED

Iacurci, Greg. 2022. "The Great Resignation Is Still in Full Swing. Here's What to Know." cnbc.com/2022. March 31. https://www.cnbc.com/2022/03/31/the -great-resignation-is-still-in-full-swing-heres-what-to-know.html.

Parker, Kim, and Juliana Menasce Horowitz. 2022. "Majority of Workers Who Quit a Job in 2021 Cite Low Pay, No Opportunities for Advancement, Feeling Disrespected." pewresearch.org/short-reads. March 9. https://www .pewresearch.org/short-reads/2022/03/09/majority-of-workers-who-quit -a-job-in-2021-cite-low-pay-no-opportunities-for-advancement-feeling -disrespected/.

Adapted from original posting as *ConsumerCorner.2022.Letter.17* (https://agribusiness.purdue.edu/consumer_corner/home-office-both -neither/)

16

THIRTY PERCENT OF NATIONALLY REPRESENTATIVE SAMPLE OF US RESIDENTS WOULD CHANGE JOBS TO OBTAIN THEIR PREFERRED WORK ARRANGEMENT

BY NICOLE J. OLYNK WIDMAR,
COURTNEY BIR, AND TORRIE SHERIDAN

We continue our exploration some of data on work-life changes stemming from the COVID-19 pandemic. In our previous book, *Consumer Corner: Markets We Thought We Knew,* we used chapter 16 to discuss pandemic-inspired workplace (or work-from-home) fashion trends, which we dubbed "Zoom-chic" (or slobbish-chic). In this book, chapter 15 looked at consumer perceptions of take-out food and travel spending pre-COVID versus in 2021. As part of that study, we asked lots of questions about their preferences for hybrid versus in-person work environments, the feasibility of working remotely based on their role, and their willingness to trade pay for flexibility—while also probing for reasons behind their preferences, such as childcare responsibilities or commuting expenses.

We thought the Great Resignation had peaked in 2021, but 2022 headlines suggested otherwise, like "The Great Resignation Is Still in Full Swing" (Iacurci 2022). In 2024, the labor market shifted yet again, with rising inflation, higher interest rates, and economic uncertainty marking the onset of what some are calling the "Great Stay" (Iacurci 2024).

Although our deep analysis was ongoing, we got the point where we were ready to share responses to a series of key questions that seemed to be gaining attention in public discourse:

1. What would your ideal work location be?
2. Would you consider leaving your current position to obtain your preferred work environment or location?
3. Would you consider taking a reduction in annual salary to obtain flexibility in work location, either at your current job or by changing jobs?
4. (Asked only to those who said "yes" to question 3) What is the maximum reduction in annual salary that you would accept in exchange for having your ideal work location, in terms of on-site versus hybrid versus remote work?

What did we find?

Only 24 percent of respondents in our nationally representative sample said their ideal working location would be exclusively remotely.

TABLE 16.1. *Ideal Work Location*

Exclusively in office	41%
Hybrid	34%
Exclusively remote	24%

When broken down by gender, a higher proportion of women preferred remote work and hybrid work compared to men.

TABLE 16.2. *Ideal Work Location by Gender*

	MALE RESPONDENTS	FEMALE RESPONDENTS
Exclusively in office	50%	34%
Hybrid	33%	36%
Exclusively remote	18%	30%

Other researchers have noted this pattern as well, citing the gender divide in remote work preferences to the unequal impacts of the pandemic and associated negative employment consequences (Pandey 2021). When asked if they would consider leaving their current position to obtain their preferred work environment, the split was nearly even among "yes," "maybe," and "no."

TABLE 16.3. *Willingness to Leave a Current Job to Obtain One in a Preferred Environment*

Would you leave your current position to obtain your preferred work environment?	
Yes	30%
Maybe	28%
No	28%
Not Applicable	14%

When investigating for men versus women, there were more men who presently worked in paid roles to whom the question was applicable. Of those men, the most selected option was "maybe," whereas for women, the most selected answer was "yes."

TABLE 16.4. *Willingness to Leave a Current Job to Obtain One in a Preferred Environment (Gender Comparison)*

Would you leave your current position to obtain your preferred work environment?		
	MALE RESPONDENTS	FEMALE RESPONDENTS
Yes	30%	31%
Maybe	33%	23%
No	28%	27%
Not Applicable	9%	19%

In total, 37% of respondents indicated they would consider taking a reduction in salary to obtain their preferred working location.

TABLE 16.5. *Willingness to Accept a Reduced Salary for a Better Work Location*

Would you accept a reduced salary for a better work location?	
Yes	37%
No	63%

More men than women indicated they would take a pay decrease to get their preferred work environment. There are likely a multitude of factors influencing willingness to take a pay cut, including present salary, earning potential in alternative positions, and the employment status of spouses or partners.

TABLE 16.6. *Willingness to Take a Reduced Salary to Obtain a Better Work Location (Gender Comparison)*

Would you accept a reduced salary for a better work location?		
	MALE RESPONDENTS	**FEMALE RESPONDENTS**
Yes	42%	33%
No	58%	67%

Among the 162 people who said they would consider taking a pay cut, the majority responded with a relatively small percentage reduction, especially considering that this was a self-reported, hypothetical scenario (which typically yields overstatements of willingness).

Further analysis was done to consider the present salary in conjunction with willingness to give up salary for flexibility or chosen work location, but suffice it to say, the enduring public discussion on *where* and *how* we work is an evolving process. It continues to shape how we interact with each other in our work and personal lives.

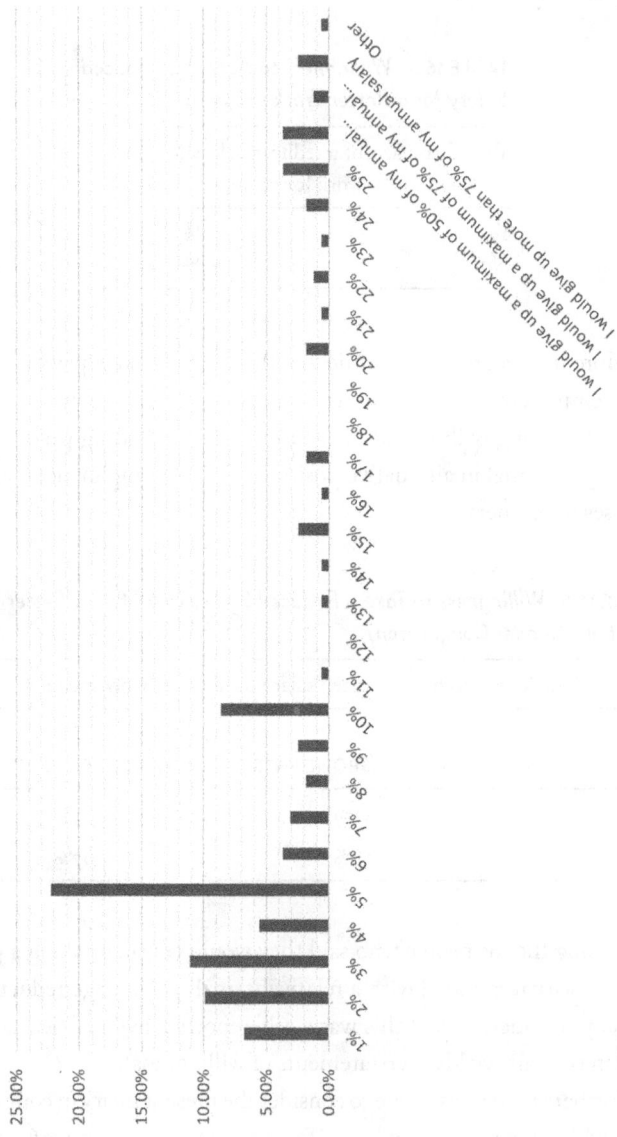

I would give up a maximum of ____ % of my annual salary to obtain my ideal work location

FIGURE 16.1. Tradeoffs of Salary and Ideal Working Location

WORKS CITED

Iacurci, Greg. 2022. "The Great Resignation Is Still in Full Swing. Here's What to Know." cnbc.com/2022. March 31. https://www.cnbc.com/2022/03/31/the-great-resignation-is-still-in-full-swing-heres-what-to-know.html.

Iacurci, Greg. 2024. "Why the 'Great Resignation' Became the 'Great Stay,' According to Labor Economists." cnbc.com/2024. December 23. https://www.cnbc.com/2024/12/23/why-the-great-resignation-became-the-great-stay-labor-economists.html.

Pandey, Erica. 2021. "The Gender Divide in Remote Work." axios.com. May 13. https://www.axios.com/2021/05/13/the-gender-divide-remote-work-men-women-childcare.

Adapted from original posting as *ConsumerCorner.2022.Letter.18* (https://agribusiness.purdue.edu/consumer_corner/nationally-representative-sample-of-us-residents-would-change-jobs-for-work-location-they-seek/)

17

LESSONS FROM STRESSED-OUT CONSUMERS SCORNED

Humans have ever-evolving tastes and preferences. Sometimes we are adventurous, eager to try new things. Other times, we most certainly are not. You may recall this from chapter 2 in our first book, *Decisions That Shape Supply Chains*, a key takeaway:

> Lesson Four: If people are coming to you for products, services, or solutions under duress, you have been given an implicit trust—treat that with great care. Pardon my language, but "Hell hath no fury like a stressed-out consumer scorned." (Widmar et al. 2025).

In the pandemic-recovery period of 2023 with talk of inflationary pressures alongside rampant levels of missed work and school due to illness (after illness, after illness, so it seems for many, especially parents), there's reason to be stressed. Especially for parents; let's get in the right mindset here as we pointed out in chapter 2 of our first book:

Parents are interesting human creatures, aren't they? One day you're eating food with a fork, maybe even while sitting down. The next thing you know, you're eating questionable leftovers while leaning over the sink (if you're lucky), without a fork in sight. . . .

As consumers, infant parents are tough, and the marketing for "baby stuff" is epically impactful (not that you can remember). Maybe it was good marketing. Or maybe you were just scared, gave up that day, and ordered what you thought your baby needed on Amazon—twice. It doesn't matter; I've been there and done that. You might have ended up with three of them and don't remember what they were. But you have three of everything in the attic now, so you must have needed it. (Widmar et al. 2025)

In the chaos of parenting during a pandemic, 2022 brought a particularly harsh blow: the infant formula shortage. Suddenly, raising a baby became exponentially more complicated. Additional findings from a study published in *Preventive Medicine Reports* helped shed light on how consumers coped. The study, conducted by Maria Kalaitzandonakes, Brenna Ellison, and Jonathan Coppess, was entitled "Coping with the 2022 Infant Formula Shortage" and was based on an online survey administered in August 2022 during the thick of the shortage.

They found that approximately 35 percent of consumers attempted to purchase formula for their own household or for someone else's during the shortage. Consumers reported searching multiple stores and sites, and in spite of warnings, some still attempted to make their own. Others relied heavily on one another to cope during the shortage, including sending and receiving formula through the mail, searching and buying for friends or relatives, and receiving it from doctors' offices or other community sources (Kalaitzandonakes et al. 2023).

Taken together, these responses raise a serious question: Are public policy efforts around child nutrition and food safety reaching people in a useful, actionable way? Warnings about what *not* to do, like making your own formula, were likely received. But without clear, viable alternatives, parents were left to sift through confusing information and misinformation during times of stress. In stressful situations, being told what *not* to do is not necessarily helpful if you're also not told what *to* do. Both analyses suggested reliance on community, friends, and family. Investments in these social safety nets are seldom spotlighted, but their importance is repeatedly highlighted and potentially deserving of additional attention in light of the public health challenges faced during a pandemic.

WORKS CITED

Kalaitzandonakes, Maria, Brenna Ellison, and Jonathan Coppess. 2023. "Coping with the 2022 Infant Formula Shortage." *Preventive Medicine Reports.*

Widmar, Nicole J. Olynk, Michael L. Smith, and Erin Robinson. 2025. "Chapter 2: Straight Talk About Consumer Behavior Under Duress." In *Decisions That Shape Supply Chains*, by Nicole J. Olynk Widmar, Michael L. Smith, and Erin Robinson. Purdue University Press.

Adapted from original posting as *ConsumerCorner.2023.Letter.06* (https://agribusiness.purdue.edu/consumer_corner/lessons-from -stressed-out-consumers-scorned/)

18

YOU, THE CONSUMER, (ALMOST CERTAINLY) DON'T KNOW WHAT YOU WANT

Building on the last chapter, try to think back—way back—to June 2020. Do you remember those days? You were wearing the newest in Zoom fashion (otherwise known as the oldest clothes you owned), with not a zipper or button in sight. You probably felt burned out. Like, really overwhelmed to the point you were too overwhelmed to notice it in the moment. It was only later, upon reflection, that you really felt the extent of the burnout. Those were hard days to navigate for many people, but grocery shopping still had to be done (somehow), and household decisions had to be made (more of them than ever!). Decisions made by consumers are made with incomplete information, abundant uncertainty, but they must continue regardless of economic, social, or cultural conditions.

Now, back to *Consumer Corner* today. The entire purpose of the series was motivated by three "repeatedly restated and largely useless conversation starters." However, I admit I was patently wrong. These are far from useless. In fact, they're problematic. They reflect flawed assumptions that deserve attention in agricultural and food industries. If we're truly seeking conversation rather than standing on a soapbox, we should be mindful and speak carefully.

With these considerations in mind, let's revisit the initial motivation for *Consumer Corner*, which were to examine these three often quoted and definitely not useless conversation starters:

- The consumer doesn't know what they want.
- The consumer doesn't understand our business.
- The consumer doesn't know they need this product yet, but they do.

Let's take them one at a time.

1. The consumer doesn't know what they want.

You don't know either! Knowing what we want is not simple. Even if we think we know today, we often change our minds once we see the next (newer? better?) option. One constant we can count on is change. Agility as a producer or supplier is key. It isn't easy, but you have to perpetually try.

2. The consumer doesn't understand our business.

It is your business, after all. None of us understand every market and every industry; most of us grasp our own field, and perhaps a few others (with varying degrees of correctness). Yet, even though we don't understand does not mean we need to be forcibly educated. That strategy is rarely effective and often off-putting. As we said before, "forcibly educating others about the product you are trying to sell them is inherently unpalatable (at best) and potentially offensive."

3. The consumer doesn't know they need this product yet, but they do.

We often try to understand what other people want before they want it. That's ambitious, considering we have a hard enough time envisioning what we want ourselves—now or tomorrow. Predicting emerging trends, staying ahead of shifting consumer desires, and meeting evolving demands are worthy goals. But telling people what they should want or need is really dangerous. Seeking to anticipate demand and meet it is one thing; declaring what's good for others or what they must have is quite another.

We all have ever-evolving tastes and preferences, yet there are times we are open to trying new things; other times, absolutely not. You may recall this from our earlier discussion about consumers under duress:

Lesson Four: If people are coming to you for products, services, or solutions under duress, you have been given an implicit trust—treat that with great care. Pardon my language, but "Hell hath no fury like a stressed-out consumer scorned." (Widmar et al. 2025)

Navigating the pandemic was tough for businesses and consumers alike. And navigating the world that followed hasn't been easy either. Inflationary pressures gave way to the desired "soft landing," avoiding a 2023 or 2024 recession. But that relief was short-lived, only to be replaced by tariff-mania and then a global trade war. Job seekers in many industries in 2024 and 2025 have encountered a frozen labor market (Karma 2025). Unsurprisingly, household financial stress is rising (Irwin 2025).

We may not always know what we want as consumers, but as producers and marketers, that uncertainty only heightens the importance of building and maintaining trust—and of communicating with care.

WORKS CITED

Irwin, Neil. 2025. "Debt Stress Signals Growing Cracks in Household Finances." axios.com/2025. March 25. https://www.axios.com/2025/03/25/consumer-confidence-debt-student-loans.

Karma, Roge. 2025. "The Job Market Is Frozen." theatlantic.com/economy. February 26. https://www.theatlantic.com/economy/archive/2025/02/jobs-unemployment-big-freeze/681831/.

Widmar, Nicole J. Olynk, Michael L. Smith, and Erin Robinson. 2025. "Chapter 2: Straight Talk About Consumer Behavior Under Duress." In *Decisions That Shape Supply Chains*, by Nicole J. Olynk Widmar, Michael L. Smith, and Erin Robinson. Purdue University Press.

Adapted from original posting as *ConsumerCorner.2023.Letter.04* (https://agribusiness.purdue.edu/consumer_corner/you-the-consumer-dont-know-what-you-want/)

CONCLUSION

Consumer Lessons From a Pandemic

O ne could hardly imagine a more obvious, and painful, lesson in how abruptly and dramatically consumer behaviors (well, all human behaviors) can change than the COVID-19 pandemic. Human behavior in everyday life is complex; far more than we often acknowledge. And because food and agriculture are essential, life-sustaining parts of our lives, these markets receive heightened attention during times of disruption.

Consumers have desires, preferences, and varying demands. But at the end of the day, everyone needs to eat. We're fickle creatures and our tastes change, and so do our interests. We discover new products, develop preferences, and sometimes fall out of love with things we once craved. But when human decision-making collides with novel threats to health, economic instability, and emotional duress, the result is anything but predictable.

In the five years since the pandemic began, we have proven to be resilient and adaptive in some ways, yet shockingly robust in resistance to change. Our daily routines like where we go, how we shop, and who we see often happen on autopilot. But in March 2020, that autopilot was switched off. What used to be a simple decision, like a quick trip to the store for milk, suddenly became a complex risk assessment: Should I go in? Will milk be available? Is it worth the exposure risk?

And then, of course, there was toilet paper, or lack thereof. Enough said.

Markets matter to us all. As we explored in *Markets We Thought We Knew*, they matter even more when they don't function flawlessly. Human nature drives us to notice the loss of something (functioning markets) more acutely than the potential for gain. Understanding how markets react to shocks, such as pandemics, supply disruptions, and trade policy shifts, is important if we hope to increase resiliency of systems like food supply chains. There is much to learn by looking back at how markets functioned through these changes in demand, supply-side shocks, and exogenous shocks. And don't forget: These weren't isolated incidents. Changes happened across overlapping time periods all while consumer behavior continued to evolve. Seasons and circumstances changed. So did we and our preferences. After all, consumers are fickle. They're demanding. They're (seemingly) uninformed.

They're you.

ABOUT THE AUTHORS

Nicole J. Olynk Widmar is an agricultural economist specializing in farm businesses and consumer decision-making under uncertainty. She serves as a professor and the head of the Department of Agricultural Economics at Purdue University.

Michael L. Smith is a research scientist specializing in the human dimensions of resource use, applying cross-disciplinary methods in agricultural economics and the social sciences. He works in Purdue University's Department of Agricultural Economics.

Erin Robinson is a communications and marketing professional with experience in agricultural business and academic research environments. As marketing manager for Purdue University's Center for Food and Agricultural Business, she develops marketing strategies, creates content and outreach initiatives, drives brand awareness, and evaluates marketing effectiveness.

ABOUT THE CONTRIBUTORS

Courtney Bir, associate professor of Agricultural Economics at Oklahoma State University, holds a PhD from Purdue and master's and bachelor's degrees from OSU. Her research examines consumer preferences for agricultural products and production economics, aiming to align preferences with profitability. Her extension work focuses on farm finance and operational goal achievement.

Torrie Sheridan is a senior writer for Purdue University, specializing in executive communications for the university's president, provost, and other leaders. In this role, she is responsible for communication plans, public relations strategies, presentations, correspondence, background briefings, and other messaging to further Purdue's land-grant mission.